Getting Started with tmux

Maximize your productivity by accessing several
terminal sessions from a single window using tmux

Victor Quinn, J.D.

open source
community experience distilled

PUBLISHING

BIRMINGHAM - MUMBAI

Getting Started with tmux

First published: September 2014

Production reference: 1170914

Published by Packt Publishing Ltd.
Livery Place
35 Livery Street
Birmingham B3 2PB, UK.

ISBN 978-1-78398-516-6

www.packtpub.com

Credits

Author

Victor Quinn, J.D.

Reviewers

Anders Damsgaard

Azat Khuzhin

Jason Lotito

Thomas Ferris Nicolaisen

Gustavo Sampaio

Ian Yang

방용배(Bang Yongbae)

Commissioning Editor

Kartikey Pandey

Acquisition Editor

Harsha Bharwani

Content Development Editor

Akshay Nair

Technical Editor

Aman Preet Singh

Copy Editors

Roshni Banerjee

Gladson Monteiro

Stuti Srivastava

Project Coordinator

Swati Kumari

Proofreaders

Ting Baker

Ameesha Green

Indexer

Tejal Soni

Graphics

Abhinash Sahu

Production Coordinator

Aparna Bhagat

Cover Work

Aparna Bhagat

About the Author

Victor Quinn, J.D., is a technology leader, programmer, and systems architect whose area of expertise is leading teams to build APIs and backend systems.

Currently, he is building the API and backend system for SocialRadar, which is a startup that builds mobile apps that provide real-time information on people around you.

Prior to joining SocialRadar, Victor led a rewriting of the financial processing online forms and APIs for NGP VAN, which is a company that processed billions of dollars in campaign contributions during the election year of 2012. The system he orchestrated is on track to process even more contributions in the coming election years. He led his team to build a system that included auto-filling and a sign-on system, enabling future contributions with a single click. All of these features were rolled up in a JavaScript single page app, making a fully functional payment processing form embeddable into even a static web page with a single tag.

He has spent many years honing his skills with command-line tools such as tmux in order to be maximally efficient in his work. His editor of choice is Emacs and he uses the Dvorak keyboard layout.

He has Bachelor of Science degrees in Physics and Computer Science from the University of Massachusetts Amherst and a Juris Doctor with focus on Intellectual Property Law from Western New England University. He is an Eagle Scout and a registered patent agent.

He lives in the Washington, D.C., metro area with his wife and Great Dane and enjoys brewing his own beer and riding his Harley.

Acknowledgments

Thank you my amazing wife, Susan, for your infinite patience and support through four-and-a-half years of working full-time while attending law school and then more years of working startup hours while undertaking innumerable side projects, including this book. Your unending support propels me and allows me to continually work toward building an awesome life for our future.

Thank you my parents, without whose support early on, I would not have become the man I am today — ever inquisitive, constantly pushing the boundaries of technology, and doing things most others do not, such as writing books like this one. I am forever grateful to you both for my excellent start in life and your loving support always!

About the Reviewers

Anders Damsgaard is a researcher at Aarhus University in Denmark, where he develops applications that simulate granular and glacier mechanics. He believes that glaciers are a key component in the climate system of the past, present, and future, and a deep understanding of their behavior is crucial in order to develop credible and reliable numerical climate models for the warm future of Earth.

In order to overcome the large computational requirements of the scientific simulations, he has turned to massively parallel modern graphics-processing units in large-scale cluster environments and has developed his own tools using primarily CUDA C and the scientific Python stack (Numpy, Scipy, and Matplotlib). The design and daily usage of high performance GNU/Linux GPU clusters have made him familiar with many modern POSIX-platform developer tools.

He has also worked with computational fluid dynamics and land surface reconstruction using the Structure-from-Motion technique, with photos taken from unmanned aerial vehicles. He is an advocate of free software and digital rights and runs a Tor relay from his home.

Azat Khuzhin is currently working on an Internet links database project, crawling websites on the Internet, and building index that currently contains more than 100 billion links. He likes to hack projects that he uses every day, for example, Linux, libevent, and others. He is keen on investigating complex issues such as when one has to go to the final software bottom layer as much as high throughput problems.

He also has his own projects, but most of them were done as research or just for fun, and they are available on his GitHub profile. He's the type of guy who runs strace if a program doesn't show normal errors on failure.

Thomas Ferris Nicolaisen is a software developer who blogs, speaks, and podcasts about tooling and techniques for programmers. He continuously keeps a check on what the great command-line utilities on all platforms are, and in doing so, he picked up tmux some years ago. Since then, he has been using and enjoying working with it for both server work and terminal windows on the desktop.

You can find his blog at www.tfnico.com and his recent podcast project on www.gitminutes.com.

Gustavo Sampaio is a software developer with different kinds of specializations. He has experience with a lot of programming languages and various platforms (Android, iOS, Windows, Linux, Web, and the microcontroller Arduino).

He has also worked with digital image processing and computer graphics, including advanced rendering techniques (global illumination, shaders, raytracing, and so on), natural language processing (the Naive Bayes classifier and POS Tagger), and parallel computing using the OpenMPI library.

He is currently studying Computer Science and has publications in his fields.

Ian Yang has several years of software development experience. Playing with various productivity tools is one of the things he loves. He is also a keyboard enthusiast who prefers to finish the job, mostly using keyboard. tmux is one of his favorite tools.

He has worked remotely for several years as a web developer. He is currently running a mobile game start-up as the co-founder and CTO.

방용배(**Bang Yongbae**) was a student of School of Computer Science and Engineering of Seoul National University in the Republic of Korea until last year. He was attracted to Ubuntu, Vim, and tmux, and therefore, he is always working with them now. He often says "black background, white text", which is the reverse of a Korean proverb.

He graduated recently and is now an intern at a small start-up, HyperConnect, that services an Android voice chat, Azar. His part is making a web tool that manages their service with Python, HTML, JavaScript, WebRTC, and WebSocket.

He will apply to graduate school next year to study more about computer science. He has big dreams, as he is young. He believes that the computer has a super power that will lead the future world. He is proud of his major and always puts on his thinking cap on how to use it effectively to make the world better.

www.PacktPub.com

Support files, eBooks, discount offers, and more

You might want to visit www.PacktPub.com for support files and downloads related to your book.

Did you know that Packt offers eBook versions of every book published, with PDF and ePub files available? You can upgrade to the eBook version at www.PacktPub.com and as a print book customer, you are entitled to a discount on the eBook copy. Get in touch with us at service@packtpub.com for more details.

At www.PacktPub.com, you can also read a collection of free technical articles, sign up for a range of free newsletters and receive exclusive discounts and offers on Packt books and eBooks.

http://PacktLib.PacktPub.com

Do you need instant solutions to your IT questions? PacktLib is Packt's online digital book library. Here, you can access, read and search across Packt's entire library of books.

Why subscribe?

- Fully searchable across every book published by Packt
- Copy and paste, print and bookmark content
- On demand and accessible via web browser

Free access for Packt account holders

If you have an account with Packt at www.PacktPub.com, you can use this to access PacktLib today and view nine entirely free books. Simply use your login credentials for immediate access.

Table of Contents

Preface

tmux is rapidly becoming the de facto standard with regards to terminal multiplexers with its breadth of features and ease of configuration. It is one of the fastest growing tools in the developer's toolkit due to its power in maximizing the productivity of a terminal window. Developers spending a large amount of time in the terminal will benefit greatly from learning how to utilize tmux and its powerful features. By taking a single terminal window and turning it into multiple windows, each with their own state, tmux is like a supercharger for your console.

We will begin with a simple introduction to tmux and learn some ways in which it can help increase productivity in your daily terminal usage. From there, we'll move on to configuring and customizing tmux to make it work, look, and feel the way that best suits your needs. Along the way, we have tutorials and screenshots aplenty so that you can follow along and avoid feeling lost. We'll also explain some of the core concepts of tmux, including the way it uses sessions, windows, and panes in order to divide content and running programs.

After learning some of these beginner topics, we will dive into some advanced tmux concepts. We'll touch on how to perform text manipulation to copy and paste text from one window to another or even to and from a file. We'll learn how to use tmux for fault-tolerant SSH sessions or pair programming, and we will finish by discussing some other open source tools that can be used alongside tmux in order to help make it even more powerful.

tmux is an incredibly capable tool, which has some concepts that can be tricky to grasp. This book will help demystify some of these tricky bits with many explanations and rich examples in a manner that cannot be found in the tmux man page.

By the end of book, you will have a much richer understanding of tmux and its capabilities and all the tools necessary to turbocharge your terminal experience. This book covers the following topics:

Chapter 1, Jump Right In, will have us really hit the ground running, taking us through a typical tmux workflow, explaining everything along the way. This allows us to experience how tmux can be useful and illustrating how it can be integrated into your daily workflow.

Chapter 2, Configuring tmux, will teach us how to change and configure almost anything about tmux's behavior, from the way it looks and feels to the commands it executes on the load. You can even configure every key combination to which tmux responds. In this chapter, we will cover the various ways to configure tmux and customize it for your workflow.

Chapter 3, Sessions, Windows, and Panes, will help us learn all about sessions, windows, and panes. These are the fundamental components that make up the window management feature of tmux and this chapter will help us understand what they are and how they relate. We will learn, through example, many ways we can work with them in order to turbocharge our terminal with tmux.

Chapter 4, Manipulating Text, helps us learn about the powerful tools of tmux for text manipulation. These tools take the form of Copy mode and paste buffers, and we will learn more about them and how to use them for very powerful text manipulation with features such as scrolling through text that has scrolled off screen and copying text from anywhere in the window history and pasting it, often without ever needing to reach for your mouse.

Chapter 5, Diving Deeper, touches on some more nuanced aspects of topics we have covered already. These topics include tmux commands and its Command mode, advanced paste buffer usage, and some advanced usage of windows and panes. We'll finish it off with learning how to launch a tmux session with some default windows.

Chapter 6, tmux for SSH, Pair Programming, and More, will walk us through a couple of usage patterns that can prove to be powerful. It will help us learn about using tmux over SSH for long-lived sessions for pair programming, and along the way, we will use Vagrant for some predictability and security.

Chapter 7, Using Other Tools with tmux, will allow us to discuss some third-party tools that can run along with tmux and add more powerful features. We'll learn about tmuxinator, which simplifies the tmux launch configuration and wemux, which brings the tmux multiuser experience to a whole new level. We'll learn about these along with a few other tricks and utilities.

Appendix contains three sections, namely *Why tmux?*, *The configuration reference*, and *Key binding and command reference*.

What you need for this book

A computer running tmux 1.8+ (Unix, Linux, or OS X) which can be downloaded from the following link:

```
http://tmux.sourceforge.net
```

Who this book is for

The book is intended for software developers, DevOps engineers, and other professionals who make heavy use of the terminal in their daily workflow. Some familiarity with the terminal is useful but no prior experience with tmux or other terminal multiplexers (such as GNU Screen) is required.

Conventions

In this book, you will find a number of styles of text that distinguish between different kinds of information. Here are some examples of these styles, and an explanation of their meaning.

When we are describing a key to press, it will appear in italics, like this: "Please press the letter *b* now" Often we will describe a key combination, which means pressing multiple keys at the same time, it will appear like this: *Ctrl* + *b*. That means hold down the Control key and press the letter b. We will also see multiple key combinations, to be pressed in series. They will appear separated by a comma and will appear like this: *Ctrl* + *b*, *c*. That means hold down the *Ctrl* key and press the letter *b*, then release both keys and press the letter *c*.

Code words in text, database table names, folder names, filenames, file extensions, pathnames, dummy URLs, user input, and Twitter handles are shown as follows: "Simply run the tmux command `show-options` with a flag for which set of options you want to view."

A block of configuration code is set as follows:

```
# Set the status bar background to blue
set-option -g status-bg blue
# Set the status bar text to white
set-option -g status-fg white

# Set the active window background in the status bar
set-window-option -g window-status-current-bg magenta
```

When we wish to draw your attention to a particular part of a code block, the relevant lines or items are set in bold:

```
# Set the active window background in the status bar
set-window-option -g window-status-current-bg magenta

# Rebind the prefix key
set-option -g prefix C-t

# Add a key binding for reloading our configuration
bind-key C-r source-file ~/.tmux.conf
```

Any command-line input or output is written as follows:

```
$ tmux attach-session -t tutorial
```

New terms and **important words** are shown in bold. Words that you see on the screen, in menus or dialog boxes for example, appear in the text like this: "You will see **Search Up:** appear in the lower left-hand corner."

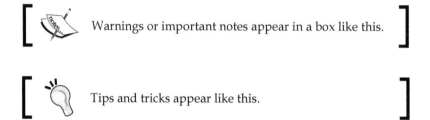

> Warnings or important notes appear in a box like this.

> Tips and tricks appear like this.

Reader feedback

Feedback from our readers is always welcome. Let us know what you think about this book—what you liked or may have disliked. Reader feedback is important for us to develop titles that you really get the most out of.

To send us general feedback, simply send an e-mail to feedback@packtpub.com, and mention the book title through the subject of your message.

You can also follow or tweet the author directly on Twitter as @victorquinn.

If there is a topic that you have expertise in and you are interested in either writing or contributing to a book, see our author guide on www.packtpub.com/authors.

Customer support

Now that you are the proud owner of a Packt book, we have a number of things to help you to get the most from your purchase.

Errata

Although we have taken every care to ensure the accuracy of our content, mistakes do happen. If you find a mistake in one of our books—maybe a mistake in the text or the code—we would be grateful if you would report this to us. By doing so, you can save other readers from frustration and help us improve subsequent versions of this book. If you find any errata, please report them by visiting http://www.packtpub.com/support, selecting your book, clicking on the **errata submission form** link, and entering the details of your errata. Once your errata are verified, your submission will be accepted and the errata will be uploaded to our website, or added to any list of existing errata, under the Errata section of that title.

Piracy

Piracy of copyright material on the Internet is an ongoing problem across all media. At Packt, we take the protection of our copyright and licenses very seriously. If you come across any illegal copies of our works, in any form, on the Internet, please provide us with the location address or website name immediately so that we can pursue a remedy.

Please contact us at copyright@packtpub.com with a link to the suspected pirated material.

We appreciate your help in protecting our authors, and our ability to bring you valuable content.

Questions

You can contact us at questions@packtpub.com if you are having a problem with any aspect of the book, and we will do our best to address it.

1
Jump Right In

Welcome! In this book, you will learn about **tmux**, a command-line program that can help maximize your productivity. It will do this by allowing you to control many virtual windows and processes from a single window, reducing your need to use your mouse and allowing you to detach and restore sessions later in the same state you left them. For more on why tmux rocks, see the *Why tmux?* section in *Appendix*.

We will eventually go over many of the concepts mentioned in this chapter in greater detail, but the best way to start getting familiar with everything is to jump right in.

So, in this chapter, we'll do just that: go on a little tour, simulate an everyday use of tmux, and point out some key concepts along the way. Fear not, if everything is not clear after the chapter, it will be covered later; this is just meant to be the first exposure.

[tmux is short for **Terminal Multiplexer**.]

Running tmux

For now, let's jump right in and start playing with it. Open up your favorite terminal application and let's get started. Just run the following command:

```
$ tmux
```

You'll probably see a screen flash, and it'll seem like not much else has happened; it looks like you're right where you were previously, with a command prompt. The word tmux is gone, but not much else appears to have changed.

However, you should notice that now there is a bar along the bottom of your terminal window. This can be seen in the following screenshot of the terminal window:

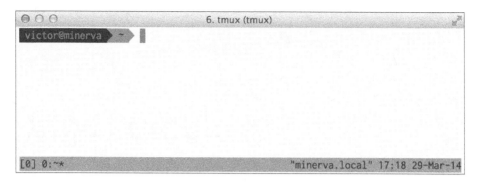

Congratulations! You're now running tmux.

That bar along the bottom is provided by tmux. We call this bar the **status line**. The status line gives you information about the session and window you are currently viewing, which other windows are available in this session, and more.

Some of what's on that line may look like gibberish now, but we'll learn more about what things mean as we progress through this book. We'll also learn how to customize the status bar to ensure it always shows the most useful items for your workflow. These customizations include things that are a part of tmux (such as the time, date, server you are connected to, and so on) or things that are in third-party libraries (such as the battery level of your laptop, current weather, or number of unread mail messages).

Sessions

By running tmux with no arguments, you create a brand new session. In tmux, the base unit is called a session. A session can have one or more windows. A window can be broken into one or more panes. We'll revisit this topic in its own whole chapter (for more information, refer to *Chapter 3, Sessions, Windows, and Panes*); however, as a sneak preview, what we have here on the current screen is a single pane taking up the whole window in a single session. Imagine that it could be split into two or more different terminals, all running different programs, and each visible split of the terminal is a pane. More on this will be covered in the later chapters.

What is a session in tmux?

It may be useful to think of a tmux session as a login on your computer.

You can log on to your computer, which initiates a new session. After you log on by entering your username and password, you arrive at an empty desktop. This is similar to a fresh tmux session. You can run one or more programs in this session, where each program has its own window or windows and each window has its own state.

In most operating systems, there is a way for you to log out, log back in, and arrive back at the same session, with the windows just as you left them. Often, some of the programs that you had opened will continue to run in the background when you log out, even though their windows are no longer visible.

A session in tmux works in much the same way. So, it may be useful to think of tmux as a mini operating system that manages running programs, windows, and more, all within a session.

You can have multiple sessions running at the same time. This is convenient if you want to have a session for each task you might be working on. You might have one for an application you are developing by yourself and another that you could use for pair programming. Alternatively, you might have one to develop an application and one to develop another. This way everything can be neat and clean and separate.

Naming the session

Each session has a name that you can set or change.

Notice the **[0]** at the very left of the status bar? This is the name of the session in brackets. Here, since you just started tmux without any arguments, it was given the name **0**. However, this is not a very useful name, so let's change it.

In the prompt, just run the following command:

```
$ tmux rename-session tutorial
```

This tells tmux that you want to rename the current session and **tutorial** is the name you'd like it to have. Of course, you can name it anything you'd like. You should see that your status bar has now been updated, so now instead of **[0]** on the left-hand side, it should now say **[tutorial]**. Here's a screenshot of my screen:

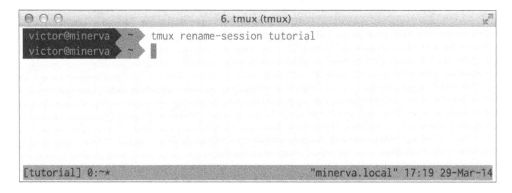

Of course, it's nice that the status bar now has a pretty name we defined rather than **0**, but it provides many more utilities than this, as we'll see in a bit!

It's worth noting that here we were giving a session a name, but this same command can also be used to rename an existing session.

The window string

The status bar has a string that represents each window to inform us about the things that are currently running. The following steps will help us to explore this a bit more:

1. Let's fire up a text editor to pretend we're doing some coding:

   ```
   $ nano test
   ```

2. Now type some stuff in there to simulate working very hard on some code:

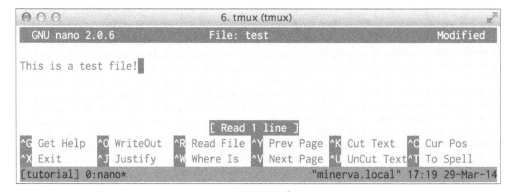

First notice how the text blob in our status bar just to the right of our session name ([**tutorial**]) has changed. It used to be **0:~*** and now it's **0:nano***. Depending on the version of tmux and your chosen shell, yours may be slightly different (for example, **0:bash***). Let's decode this string a bit.

This little string encodes a lot of information, some of which is provided in the following bullet points:

- The zero in the front represents the number of the window. As we'll shortly see, each window is given a number that we can use to identify and switch to it.

- The colon separates the window number from the name of the program running in that window.

- The symbols ~ or **nano** in the previous screenshot are loosely names of the running program. We say "loosely" because you'll notice that ~ is not the name of a program, but was the directory we were visiting. tmux is pretty slick about this; it knows some state of the program you're using and changes the default name of the window accordingly. Note that the name given is the default; it's possible to explicitly set one for the window, as we'll see later.

- The symbol * indicates that this is the currently viewed window. We only have one at the moment, so it's not too exciting; however, once we get more than one, it'll be very helpful.

Creating another window

OK! Now that we know a bit about a part of the status line, let's create a second window so we can run a terminal command. Just press *Ctrl + b*, then *c*, and you will be presented with a new window!

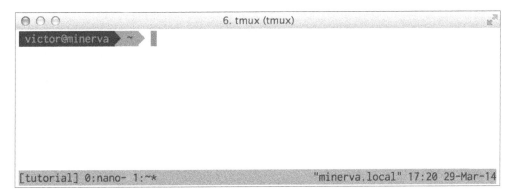

A few things to note are as follows:

- Now there is a new window with the label **1:~***. It is given the number 1 because the last one was 0. The next will be 2, then 3, 4, and so on.

- The asterisk that denoted the currently active window has been moved to 1 since it is now the active one.

- The nano application is still running in window 0.

- The asterisk on window 0 has been replaced by a hyphen (**-**). The **-** symbol denotes the previously opened window. This is very helpful when you have a bunch of windows.

Let's run a command here just to illustrate how it works. Run the following commands:

```
$ echo "test" > test
```

```
$ cat test
```

The output of these commands can be seen in the following screenshot:

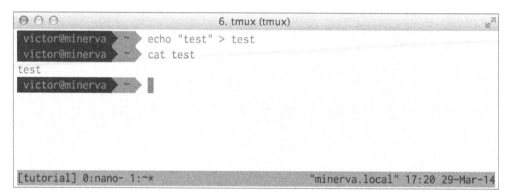

This is just some stuff so we can help identify this window. Imagine in the real world though you are moving a file, performing operations with Git, viewing log files, running top, or anything else.

Let's jump back to window 0 so we can see nano still running. Simply press *Ctrl + b* and *l* to switch back to the previously opened window (the one with the hyphen; *l* stands for the last). As shown in the following screenshot, you'll see that nano is alive, and well, it looks exactly as we left it:

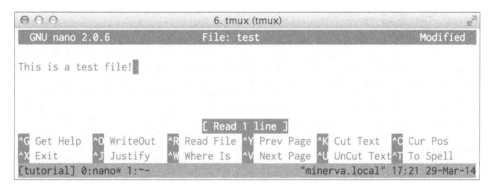

The prefix key

There is a special key in tmux called the **prefix key** that is used to perform most of the keyboard shortcuts. We have even used it already quite a bit! In this section, we will learn more about it and run through some examples of its usage.

You will notice that in the preceding exercise, we pressed *Ctrl + b* before creating a window, then *Ctrl + b* again before switching back, and *Ctrl + b* before a number to jump to that window.

When using tmux, we'll be pressing this key a lot. It's even got a name! We call it the prefix key. Its default binding in tmux is *Ctrl + b*, but you can change that if you prefer something else or if it conflicts with a key in a program you often use within tmux. You can send the *Ctrl + b* key combination through to the program by pressing *Ctrl + b* twice in a row; however, if it's a keyboard command you use often, you'll most likely want to change it. This key is used before almost every command we'll use in tmux, so we'll be seeing it a lot.

From here on, if we need to reference the prefix key, we'll do it like <Prefix>. This way if you rebind it, the text will still make sense. If you don't rebound it or see <Prefix>, just type *Ctrl + b*.

Let's create another window for another task. Just run <Prefix>, *c* again. Now we've got three windows: 0, 1, and 2. We've got one running nano and two running shells, as shown in the following screenshot:

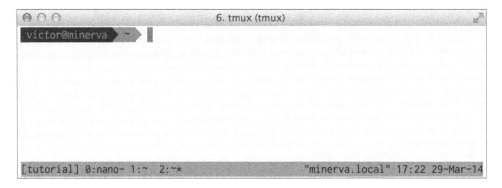

Some more things to note are as follows:

- Now we have window 2, which is active. See the asterisk?
- Window 0 now has a hyphen because it was the last window we viewed.
- This is a clear, blank shell because the one we typed stuff into is over in Window 1.

Let's switch back to window 1 to see our test commands above still active. The last time we switched windows, we used <Prefix>, *l* to jump to the last window, but that will not work to get us to window 1 at this point because the hyphen is on window 0. So, going to the last selected window will not get us to 1.

Thankfully, it is very easy to switch to a window directly by its number. Just press <Prefix>, then the window number to jump to that window. So <Prefix>, *1* will jump to window 1 even though it wasn't the last one we opened, as shown in the following screenshot:

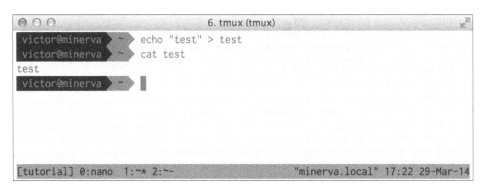

Sure enough, now window 1 is active and everything is present, just as we left it. Now we typed some silly commands here, but it could just as well have been an active running process here, such as unit tests, code linting, or top. Any such process would run in the background in tmux without an issue.

This is one of the most powerful features of tmux.

In the traditional world, to have a long-running process in a terminal window and get some stuff done in a terminal, you would need two different terminal windows open; if you accidentally close one, the work done in that window will be gone.

tmux allows you to keep just one terminal window open, and this window can have a multitude of different windows within it, closing all the different running processes. Closing this terminal window won't terminate the running processes; tmux will continue humming along in the background with all of the programs running behind the scenes.

Help on key bindings

Now a keen observer may notice that the trick of entering the window number will only work for the first 10 windows. This is because once you get into double digits, tmux won't be able to tell when you're done entering the number. If this trick of using the prefix key plus the number only works for the first 10 windows (windows 0 to 9), how will we select a window beyond 10?

Thankfully, tmux gives us many powerful ways to move between windows. One of my favorites is the **choose window** interface.

However, oh gee! This is embarrassing. Your author seems to have entirely forgotten the key combination to access the choose window interface. Don't fear though; tmux has a nice built-in way to access all of the key bindings. So let's use it!

Press <Prefix>, ? to see your screen change to show a list with *bind-key* to the left, the key binding in the middle, and the command it runs to the right. You can use your arrow keys to scroll up and down, but there are a lot of entries there!

Thankfully, there is a quicker way to get to the item you want without scrolling forever.

Press *Ctrl + s* and you'll see a prompt appear that says **Search Down:**, where you can type a string and it will search the help document for that string.

Emacs or vi mode

tmux tries hard to play nicely with developer defaults, so it actually includes two different modes for many key combinations tailored for the two most popular terminal editors: Emacs and vi. These are referred to in tmux parlance as status-keys and mode-keys that can be either Emacs or vi.

The tmux default mode is Emacs for all the key combinations, but it can be changed to vi via configuration, something we'll cover in *Chapter 2, Configuring tmux*. It may also be set to vi automatically based on the global $EDITOR setting in your shell.

If you are used to Emacs, *Ctrl + s* should feel very natural since it's the command Emacs uses to search.

So, if you try *Ctrl + s* and it has no effect, your keys are probably in the vi mode. We'll try to provide guidance when there is a mode-specific key like this by including the vi mode's counterpart in parentheses after the default key.

For example, in this case, the command would look like *Ctrl + s* (/) since the default is *Ctrl + s* and / is the command in the vi mode.

Type in `choose-window` and hit *Enter* to search down and find the `choose-window` key binding. Oh look! There it is; it's **w**:

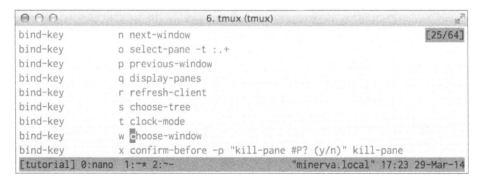

However, what exactly does that mean?

Well, all that means is that we can type our prefix key (<Prefix>), followed by the key in that help document to run the mentioned command. First, let's get out of these help docs. To get out of these or any screens like them, generated by tmux, simply press *q* for quit and you should be back in the shell prompt for window 2.

If you ever forget any key bindings, this should be your first step.

A nice feature of this key binding help page is that it is dynamically updated as you change your key bindings.

Later, when we get to **Configuration**, you may want to change bindings or bind new shortcuts. They'll all show up in this interface with the configuration you provide them with.

Can't do that with manpages!

Now, to open the choose window interface, simply type <Prefix>, *w* since *w* was the key shown in the help bound to **choose-window** and voilà:

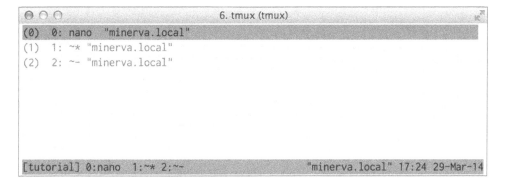

Notice how it nicely lays out all of the currently open windows in a task-manager-like interface.

It's interactive too. You can use the arrow keys to move up and down to highlight whichever window you like and then just hit *Enter* to open it. Let's open the window with nano running. Move up to highlight window 0 and hit *Enter*.

You may notice a few more convenient and intuitive ways to switch between the currently active windows when browsing through the key bindings help. For example, <Prefix>, *p* will switch to the previous window and <Prefix>, *n* will switch to the next window. Whether refreshing your recollection on a key binding you've already learnt or seeking to discover a new one, the key bindings help is an excellent resource.

Searching for text

Now we only have three windows so it's pretty easy to remember what's where, but what if we had 30 or 300? With tmux, that's totally possible. (Though, this is not terribly likely or useful! What would you do with 300 active windows?)

One other convenient way to switch between windows is to use the **find-window** feature. This will prompt us for some text, and it will search all the active windows and open the window that has the text in it.

If you've been following along, you should have the window with nano currently open (window 0). Remember we had a shell in window 1 where we had typed some silly commands? Let's try to switch to that one using the **find-window** feature.

Type <Prefix>, *f* and you'll see a **find-window** prompt as shown in the following screenshot:

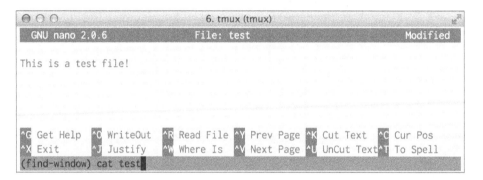

Here, type in `cat test` and hit *Enter*.

You'll see you've switched to window 1 because it had the `cat test` command in it.

However, what if you search for some text that is ambiguous? For example, if you've followed along, you will see the word `test` appear multiple times on both windows 0 and 1. So, if you try **find-window** with just the word `test`, it couldn't magically switch right away because it wouldn't know which window you mean.

Thankfully, tmux is smart enough to handle this. It will give you a prompt, similar to the *choose-window* interface shown earlier, but with only the windows that match the query (in our case, windows 0 and 1; window 2 did not have the word test in it). It also includes the first line in each window (for context) that had the text.

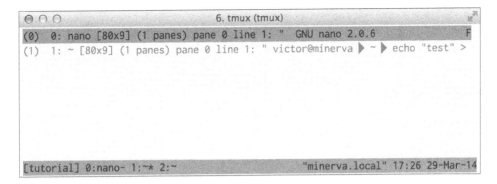

Pick window 0 to open it.

Detaching and attaching

Now press <Prefix>, *d*.

Uh oh! Looks like tmux is gone! The familiar status bar is no more available. The <Prefix> key set does nothing anymore.

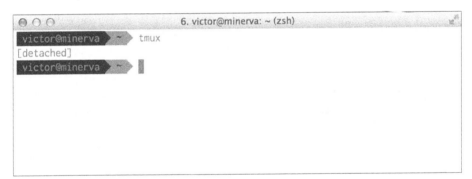

You may think we the authors have led you astray, causing you to lose your work. What will you do without that detailed document you were writing in nano?

Fear not explorer, we are simply demonstrating another very powerful feature of tmux. <Prefix>, *d* will simply detach the currently active session, but it will keep running happily in the background!

Yes, although it looks like it's gone, our session is alive and well.

How can we get back to it? First, let's view the active sessions. In your terminal, run the following command:

```
$ tmux list-sessions
```

You should see a nice list that has your session name, number of windows, and date of creation and dimensions. If you had more than one session, you'd see them here too.

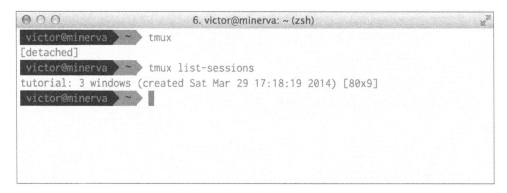

To re attach the detached session to your session, simply run the following command:

```
$ tmux attach-session -t tutorial
```

This tells tmux to attach a session and the session to attach it to as the target (hence -t). In this case, we want to attach the session named **tutorial**. Sure enough, you should be back in your tmux session, with the now familiar status bar along the bottom and your nano masterpiece back in view.

Note that this is the most verbose version of this command. You can actually omit the target if there is only one running session, as is in our scenario. This shortens the command to tmux attach-session. It can be further shortened because attach-session has a shorter alias, attach. So, we could accomplish the same thing with just tmux attach.

Throughout this text, we will generally use the more verbose version, as they tend to be more descriptive, and leave shorter analogues as exercises for the reader.

Explaining tmux commands

Now you may notice that attach-session sounds like a pretty long command. It's the same as list-sessions, and there are many others in the lexicon of tmux commands that seem rather verbose.

Tab completion

There is less complexity to the long commands than it may seem because most of them can be tab-completed. Try going to your command prompt and typing the following:

```
$ tmux list-se
```

Next, hit the *Tab* key. You should see it fill out to this:

```
$ tmux list-sessions
```

So thankfully, due to tab completion, there is little need to remember these long commands.

Note that tab completion will only work in certain shells with certain configurations, so if the tab completion trick doesn't work, you may want to search the Web and find a way to enable tab completion for tmux.

Aliases

Most of the commands have an alias, which is a shorter form of each command that can be used. For example, the alias of list-sessions is ls. The alias of new-session is new.

You can see them all readily by running the tmux command list-commands (alias lscm), as used in the following code snippet:

```
$ tmux list-commands
```

This will show you a list of all the tmux commands along with their aliases in parenthesis after the full name.

Throughout this text, we will always use the full form for clarity, but you could just as easily use the alias (or just tab complete of course).

One thing you'll most likely notice is that only the last few lines are visible in your terminal. If you go for your mouse and try to scroll up, that won't work either! How can you view the text that is placed above? We will need to move into something called the Copy mode that has its own chapter later in this text (See *Chapter 4, Manipulating Text*).

Renaming windows

Let's say you want to give a more descriptive name to a window. If you had three different windows, each with the nano editor open, seeing nano for each window wouldn't be all that helpful.

Thankfully, it's very easy to rename a window. Just switch to the window you'd like to rename. Then <Prefix>, , will prompt you for a new name. Let's rename the nano window to masterpiece.

See how the status line has been updated and now shows window **0** with the **masterpiece** title as shown in the following screenshot. Thankfully, tmux is not smart enough to check the contents of your window; otherwise, we're not sure whether the masterpiece title would make it through.

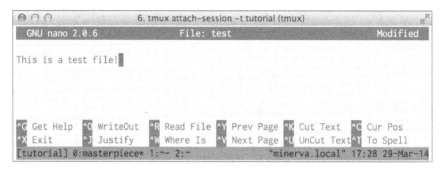

Killing windows

As the last stop on our virtual tour, let's kill a window we no longer need. Switch to window 1 with our find-window trick by entering <Prefix>, *f*, cat test, *Enter* or of course we could use the less exciting <Prefix>, *l* command to move to the last opened window.

Now let's say goodbye to this window. Press <Prefix>, *&* to kill it. You will receive a prompt to which you have to confirm that you want to kill it.

This is a destructive process, unlike detaching, so be sure anything you care about has been saved.

Once you confirm it, window 1 will be gone. Poor window 1! You will see that now there are only window 0 and window 2 left:

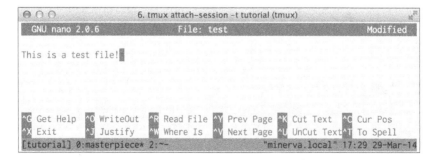

You will also see that now <Prefix>, *f*, cat test, *Enter* no longer loads window 1 but rather says **No windows matching: cat test**. So, window 1 is really no longer with us.

Whenever we create a new window, it will take the lowest available index, which in this case will be 1. So window 1 can rise again, but this time as a new and different window with little memory of its past. We can also renumber windows as we'll see later, so if window 1 being missing is offensive to your sense of aesthetics, fear not, it can be remedied!

Summary

In this chapter, we got to jump right in and get a whirlwind tour of some of the coolest features in tmux.

Here is a quick summary of the features we covered in this chapter:

- Starting tmux
- Naming and renaming sessions
- The window string and what each chunk means
- Creating new windows
- The prefix key
- Multiple ways to switch back and forth between windows
- Accessing the help documents for available key bindings
- Detaching and attaching sessions
- Renaming and killing windows

In the next chapter, we will look into configuration and many of the ways tmux can be customized to fit your tastes and workflow.

For a reference of all the commands learned in this chapter and every following chapter, you can refer to the *Key binding and command reference* section in *Appendix*.

2
Configuring tmux

Now that we've had our first taste of tmux, let's dig into our first topic in greater detail. tmux is a very powerful program and thankfully one that is also highly configurable. You can change almost anything about its behavior, from the way it looks and feels to the commands it executes on load; you can even configure every key combination to which tmux responds.

In this chapter, we will cover various ways to configure tmux to customize and optimize it for your workflow. We will build a sample configuration that can be used to make tmux a bit cleaner, prettier, and more useful.

We will be unable to cover every minute detail or configuration option, but we will hit the most common ones and set you up with the knowledge and toolset to be able to tackle any configuration you desire. In this chapter, we will discuss the following:

- Using the set-option command
- Creating a tmux configuration file
- Emacs or vi mode
- Enabling mouse modes
- Changing the status bar
    - Modifying the background color of the status bar
    - Reloading the configuration
    - Changing the foreground color of the status bar
    - Highlighting the active window

- Binding keys
    - Viewing current bindings
    - Chaining multiple commands to a single key
    - Comments in the configuration file
    - Rebinding the prefix key

- Binding a new prefix key
- Binding keys without the prefix key
- Unbinding keys
- Revising the status bar
- Option types
- Handy configuration tips

By the end of this chapter, we will also have built up a sample configuration file that you can use as a starting point for your own personalized configuration.

Using the set-option command

The main way in which options are set and configured within tmux is through the appropriately named set-option command.

This command can be called on its own to set an option temporarily. However, most of the time, we will use it to set options within a tmux configuration file so each time we launch tmux, the options are set the way we would like.

For a taste of using the set-option command to set an option temporarily, open a terminal window and launch tmux; alternatively, if you've been following along through *Chapter 1, Jump Right In*, just type the following command in the window:

```
$ tmux set-option status off
```

Once you do this, the status bar will disappear! This setting is only temporary, so if you leave it as is, end the session, and restart tmux or create a new session, it will not load this setting. In other words, a status bar will appear.

What you have done is that you've told tmux to set the option status to a value of off. You can use this command to set any tmux option on the fly in this manner. Having no status bar can be a bit unsettling, so let's turn it back on:

```
$ tmux set-option status on
```

If we want these configuration options to persist through tmux restarts and sessions, we need some way to tell tmux what their values should be. We will do that by creating a tmux configuration file.

Creating a tmux configuration file

In order to keep the settings around after restarting tmux, we will create a configuration file that will include all the information about what options we want to set and to what values.

Like many other Unix-based utilities, configuring tmux is as simple as creating a file with the name .tmux.conf in your home directory.

However, unlike many other configuration files, a tmux configuration file does not contain some kind of specific configuration language for the program, rather it consists of a series of tmux commands that are run, in order, when tmux starts up. Most of the commands we'll see are simple set-option commands similar to the commands we played with in the previous examples. Let's create and start building our configuration file:

```
$ cd ~
$ touch .tmux.conf
```

Open this newly created file in your favorite text editor and we're ready to rock!

Like with most Unix-based utilities, this file in your personal directory contains the configuration for your user only.

It is also possible to set the global tmux configuration that will apply to all the users in the system. It follows the same format as that of a personal configuration file but generally lives in /etc/tmux.conf.

However, since it is likely that not all the users of a system want the same global configuration, it's probably best to just modify your own personal configuration.

Emacs or vi mode

As we discovered in *Chapter 1*, *Jump Right In*, tmux tries to help developers by providing two sets of key bindings, one each for the two most widespread text editors. If you swing one way or the other, this is likely to be one of the first things you'll want to change to make tmux feel right for you.

The default for tmux is to use the Emacs mode keys, so if you are an Emacs user, you may be all set. tmux also tries to help out and might, based on environment variables, switch to one group or the other by default. To check which mode tmux is currently in, run the following command:

```
$ tmux show-options -g | grep key
```

You should get an output that looks something similar to the following command:

```
$ status-keys emacs
```

If you are in the mode you'd like to be in, you can do nothing. If you are in the wrong mode though, you would most likely want to add the following couple of lines to your .tmux.conf file, obviously choosing the appropriate editor:

```
set-option -g status-keys emacs
set-option -g mode-keys emacs
```

This will allow you to use the shortcut keys you are most familiar with in many of the modes throughout tmux.

Enabling mouse modes

First, it's worthwhile to note that one of the main benefits of tmux is to obviate the need to reach for your mouse as often as you otherwise would. So, some purists would balk at the notion of enabling mouse modes for tmux.

That said, it is often rather convenient to use the mouse to scroll, select text, resize panes, choose an option from a list, and more. And yes, tmux allows you to do all of that with the mouse. These features are disabled by default so to enable them, we need to add the following lines to our .tmux.conf (either Emacs or vi):

```
set-window-option -g mouse-mode on
set-option -g mouse-select-window on
set-option -g mouse-select-pane on
set-option -g mouse-resize-pane on
```

This will enable mouse functionality in all of the ways we described. We haven't yet dealt with panes, but when we touch on that in *Chapter 3, Sessions, Windows, and Panes*, it will be more apparent how using the mouse to resize them will be incredibly convenient.

Changing the status bar

We learned a bit about the status bar in the last chapter when we discussed changing the session and window names. This status bar is highly customizable, and it's a great place to start learning about configuring tmux. We can change the status bar colors, what appears on the status bar, the alignment, and much more.

Modifying the background color of the status bar

Let's add an item to our configuration to change the color of the status bar. As we saw by jumping in, the default color of the status bar is a shade of green. Note that there happens to be a shade of green in our configuration as well, but it is likely a different color on your terminal unless you are using the same color scheme as we are.

 The authors are using a color scheme called Solarized. It is a color scheme that includes both dark and light variants and is optimized for the terminal and readability. It was developed by Ethan Schoonover and has gained quite a following in the tech community for its precision, symmetry, and because it makes just about any code look downright pretty. For more information, visit http://ethanschoonover.com/solarized.

The color scheme of our current terminal is as shown in the following screenshot:

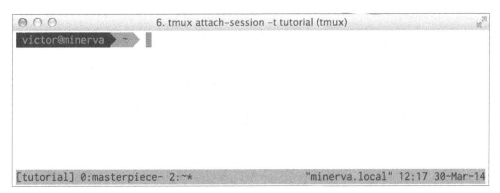

Eeek! That's pretty ugly with our current color scheme.

Say, we want it to be a nicer blue color. Jump into your favorite text editor and edit ~/.tmux.conf to have the following line:

```
set-option -g status-bg blue
```

This line specifies that we want the status bar to be blue rather than its default, which on our system happened to be green.

Let's break this line apart and explain it a bit:

- `set-option`: We want to set an option. This command has a shorter alias `set`, which may be preferred.

- `-g`: This means this option should be applied globally. It is actually possible to set many options (such as the status bar's color) on a per-window basis if desired.

- `status-bg`: This is the option we are setting. In this case, we are setting the status's background color.

- `blue`: This is the value we are using on which variable. We want a blue background. The allowed color values are:

  - Named colors, such as `black`, `red`, `green`, `yellow`, `blue`, `magenta`, `cyan`, or `white`

  - `colour0` to `colour255` (where the number is 0 to 255 on a 256-color palette)

  - A hex value such as `#ff0000`

  - `default`

Unlike on the Web, a particular color code doesn't necessarily mean the same thing in every terminal.

Some terminals support the full xterm palette of 256 colors, some only support 16, and some don't support any colors. Most have their own flavor of colors due to terminal color themes, so what you specify as blue may not be rendered on the screen as blue at all.

For example, using the previously mentioned Solarized color theme, specifying the color of `#00ff00` (which is the hex code for pure green) will actually be rendered on the screen with a hex value of `#859900`, a kind of pea soup green optimized to match the Solarized color theme.

However, most of the time, red is some shade of red, green is some shade of green, and so on; therefore, for our purposes, we'll use these simple primary colors and assume your terminal will be getting it somewhat close.

Recall how we said previously that the items in this configuration file are full-fledged tmux commands? We can put that to the test right now. Jump to your terminal window, get to a window with a shell (instead of your editor), and run the following command:

```
$ tmux set-option -g status-bg red
```

You should see your status bar change to red immediately (again, depending on the color capabilities of your shell and terminal program).

Notice that all we did was take the same text we put in our configuration file, type it after `tmux`, and we were good to go.

Recall that any command run in the shell like this is only temporary, so we still want our configuration file; however, this is a nice way to quickly test that a given command is going to work as we'd like.

Reloading the configuration

Now we have a shiny new configuration file with our new command to change the color of the status bar, but this configuration is useless until we reload the configuration to tell tmux to load with the commands from our new file.

After you save your configuration file, it's ready for action, but look, your status bar is still green! How do we tell tmux that it should go fetch the latest configuration and reload the windows to use that configuration? There are two ways to tell tmux to reload the configuration.

The first is to kill all the sessions entirely and start tmux fresh. This is not a very appealing option because it entails closing all of our tmux sessions, which in turn means closing all the currently open and running programs. We will then have to reinitiate all of our tmux sessions and windows and restart all of our programs to get back to where we were before just to reload the configuration. It works but is a rather messy solution overall. Generally, it is rather nice that tmux loads the new configuration file when it is restarted because this means any subsequent tmux initiation will use our latest configuration, which makes sense. However, it forces us to close all the running applications to load it, which is not ideal.

The second, more common and useful option is to use the tmux `source-file` command. This command will tell tmux to go fetch the latest configuration and load it immediately. In this case, there is no need to leave tmux!

Get to a command-line prompt within tmux (if you followed along *Chapter 1, Jump Right In*, you will know that you can just hit <Prefix>, 2 to bring up the command prompt we left there). If you have no window currently open, just open a new window within tmux (<Prefix>, *c*) and it'll start with a command prompt by default. Now type the following command in the prompt and hit *Enter*:

```
$ tmux source-file ~/.tmux.conf
```

Similar to the following screenshot, you should see the status bar is now blue!

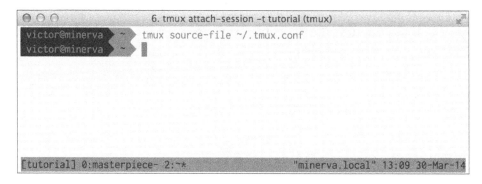

Changing the foreground color of the status bar

Now the blue status bar looks nice! However, the text is a bit difficult to read; there's not much of a contrast between the background and the text. Let's fix that!

Open the `.tmux.conf` file again, this time adding the second line:

```
set-option -g status-bg blue
set-option -g status-fg white
```

Reload the configuration with the `source-file` command using the method we discussed previously. Now, as can be seen in the following screenshot, the text on the status bar should be much more readable!

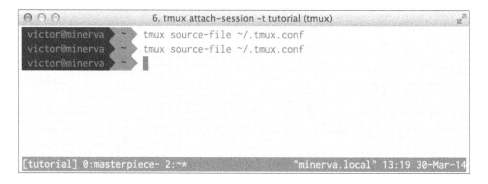

Highlighting the active window

Let's make it a bit easier to see which is our currently active window. The asterisk works, but it could be a bit easier since we have these colors.

Open up the `.tmux.conf` file again, and this time add the third line:

```
set-option -g status-bg blue
set-option -g status-fg white
set-window-option -g window-status-current-bg magenta
```

Here we see our first window option. The first two options were global. This means that in all windows the status bar will always have a blue background.

This new line is saying that, for each window, if it is the current window, set its background to `magenta`. Reload the configuration again with `tmux source-file ~/.tmux.conf` to see that in action, as shown in the following screenshot:

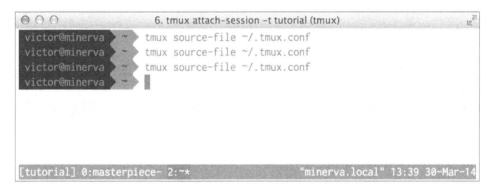

Change to the other window and watch the magenta highlight follow.

You may be noticing that each time, we're typing a lot to reload this configuration, going through the whole `tmux source-file ~/.tmux.conf` command. Surely, there must be a better way!

The bad news is that there is not a key combination out of the box in tmux to reload the configuration. The good news is that we can bind our own key to make this task easier!

Binding keys

Binding keys will allow you to change the keys and key combinations that tmux will recognize for any command. This also allows us to create new key combinations for existing commands or change the key binding for any existing keys used by tmux. It even lets you assign new key bindings to any command we can dream about.

The commands to which we can bind keys can even prompt for user input. There is no constraint on uniqueness, so we could bind multiple keys to issue the same command or bind no keys for a particular command.

What this all means is that while there is not an existing key combination available to reload the tmux source file, we can make up our own key combination and assign it to the rather lengthy `source-file` command so we don't have to type the whole thing each time we want to reload the configuration.

First, let's find a good key combination to bind for this command.

Viewing current bindings

Recall from the first chapter that we were able to see all of the current key bindings by issuing <Prefix>, ?. This is actually the keyboard shortcut for the `list-keys` command. This shows all of the current key bindings within tmux and is nicely updated whenever we reload the configuration.

This is a very helpful resource if you forget key bindings, but it's also useful as a heads-up view of which keys are already currently used for bindings. Any keys not listed here are not currently bound to anything in tmux, so they are fair game for new uses. Here's a screenshot on the current bindings:

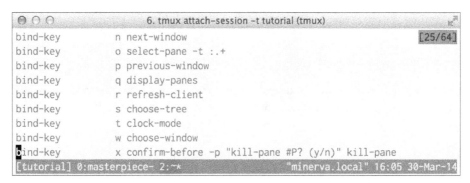

Unfortunately, an easy and memorable choice, r is taken by `refresh-client`. We could override this; it is not often used, but let us find one that's not used.

Thankfully, by looking through the list of key bindings, it appears that *Ctrl + r* is not currently bound to any tmux command. So it's fair game. All the keys that start with **C-** in the key binding screen mean that you need to press the *Ctrl* key. So, `c-r` is used in the same way as *Ctrl + r*.

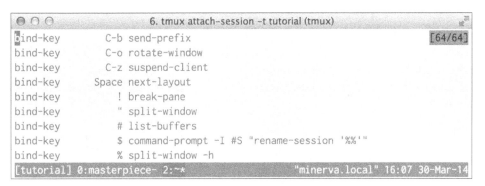

This will be rather convenient as the default prefix key also uses the *Ctrl* key. So assuming the current default prefix key of *Ctrl + b*, we will be able to hold down *Ctrl* and tap *B* then *R* to reload the configuration.

Rebinding Ctrl to Caps Lock

One of my favorite programming productivity tips of all time is to rebind *Caps Lock* to *Ctrl* on a system-wide scale. This is easily done on most computers at the operating system level and even on some more capable keyboards.

The majority of computer users seldom use *Caps Lock*, yet its place on the home row makes it a convenient key to press. Since *Ctrl* is used often by command-line programmers and its place on the keyboard is rather difficult to press, swapping the two can be very helpful. By swapping them, in the unlikely event that you ever do need to use *Caps Lock*, it is still accessible by the old *Ctrl* key on your keyboard.

The author is a huge fan of Emacs that makes heavy use of the *Ctrl* key, and tmux is another program that does as well.

This is by no means a requirement, but if you find yourself using the *Ctrl* key regularly, consider making use of this trick!

On a Mac, it is very easy and requires no additional software. It's a bit trickier on some other systems, but possible everywhere.

For detailed tutorials visit `http://vq.io/rebindcaps`.

So let's add a key binding for *Ctrl + r* to reload our configuration. Reopen your .tmux.conf file and add the fourth line:

```
set-option -g status-bg blue
set-option -g status-fg white
set-window-option -g window-status-current-bg magenta
bind-key C-r source-file ~/.tmux.conf
```

Notice that the format of this new bind-key row is very similar to what we saw in the key bindings list. Interestingly, each row in the key bindings is a verbatim key binding so we can copy and paste it into our .tmux.conf file, and it will just work. This is very convenient!

Let's break this bind-key line apart and explain it a bit:

- bind-key: We want to bind a key.
- C-r: The key combination we want to bind is *Ctrl + r*.
- source-file ~/.tmux.conf: Upon pressing that key combination, we want to run the source-file command and provide it with the path to our source file as an argument.
- It is worth noting that, similar to the way we put commands in the tmux configuration file and they would be if run from the command line after the tmux keyword, the bind-key syntax also drops the tmux but otherwise is a valid tmux command.

Now we will need to reload our configuration once in the old way before we can use our keyboard combination:

```
$ tmux source-file ~/.tmux.conf
```

That's it! From here on, we can press <Prefix>, then *Ctrl + r*, and the configuration will be reloaded.

Sure enough, if we look at our current key bindings as we did before with the <Prefix>, *?* key combination, we'll find that our new binding to reload the source file, which is bound to **C-r**, will be right at the top of the screen:

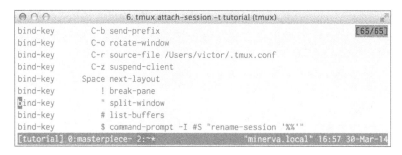

Chaining multiple commands to a single key

You may notice that, while we can inspect the key bindings to see that the configuration was reloaded, we otherwise will get no visual indication that things have been updated and the configuration reloaded. This is because the `source-file` command outputs nothing when it does its job.

There isn't much we can do to change this behavior directly. Thankfully though tmux does give us a way to chain together multiple commands to a single key binding.

This will allow us to chain two commands, in this case, the `source-file` command we currently have and a command to display some text to give us some feedback that the file has been reloaded.

Reopening our trusty configuration file, change the last line as follows:

```
set-option -g status-bg blue
set-option -g status-fg white
set-window-option -g window-status-current-bg magenta
bind-key C-r source-file ~/.tmux.conf; display "reloaded!"
```

Now *Ctrl + r* will run both the `source-file` command and the `display` command to let us know that it has done its job! This could be used to chain any multiple commands you desire. Save the file, exit your editor (or switch to another window leaving your editor running!), and reload your configuration with <Prefix>, *Ctrl + r* and you should see the text **reloaded!** flash in the status bar momentarily.

Comments in the configuration file

OK, so now our configuration is up to four lines, and it's getting a bit unwieldy without any comments or anything for guidance. Thankfully, we can add arbitrary comments to our `.tmux.conf` file with ease. Just start the line with a hashtag (#).

So let's jazz up our `.tmux.conf` file with some nice comments to explain what we're doing:

```
# Set the status bar background to blue
set-option -g status-bg blue
# Set the status bar text to white
set-option -g status-fg white

# Set the active window background in the status bar
set-window-option -g window-status-current-bg magenta

# Add a key binding for reloading our configuration
bind-key C-r source-file ~/.tmux.conf
```

Notice how we also added some spaces between some logical groupings here as well. Thankfully, the tmux configuration ignores whitespace so we can space them apart however we'd like.

Binding a new prefix key

We can also rebind the prefix key to make it something more convenient or set it up in a way that it doesn't get into a conflict with other programs.

Some of you might be from a background where you use GNU screen, another terminal multiplexer that uses *Ctrl + a* as its prefix key. So instead of learning the tmux key, you might want to simply rebind *Ctrl + a* as your tmux prefix key.

Alternatively, you might be a frequent user of Emacs, nano, or another program that makes extensive use of *Ctrl + b* to move the point back one character. In that case, *Ctrl + b* is not a convenient key to have rebound globally.

Users in this category may choose to rebind the prefix to something less used or less important in Emacs or other programs, such as *Ctrl + t*. This also conveniently helps to provide guidance on the key (*t* for tmux!).

Whatever your motives, it is possible to rebind the prefix key. So, as an exercise, let's rebind it to *Ctrl + t*. If this makes you uncomfortable, feel free to ignore it in your own configuration. However, rebinding the prefix key is a bit different than rebinding any other key. You might think that the following in your `.tmux.conf` file would work, but that is *not* the case:

```
bind-key C-t prefix
```

Recall that all of the key bindings within tmux first require the prefix key to work. So this code snippet, in plain English, is essentially saying, "After you have pressed the prefix key, press *Ctrl* and *t* as the prefix key." It is not saying, "Here is the new prefix key, please use it."

So in order to set the prefix key, add the following lines to our ever-growing `.tmux.conf`:

```
# Set the status bar background to blue
set-option -g status-bg blue
# Set the status bar text to white
set-option -g status-fg white
```

```
# Set the active window background in the status bar
set-window-option -g window-status-current-bg magenta

# Rebind the prefix key
set-option -g prefix C-t

# Add a key binding for reloading our configuration
bind-key C-r source-file ~/.tmux.conf
```

This will actually change the prefix key. Assuming you still have the default prefix key of *Ctrl + b*, try reloading your configuration using *Ctrl + b, Ctrl + r*, using *Ctrl + b* as the prefix key for the last time to load our configuration. If you have already changed your prefix key, you might need to use a different key combination.

Now press *Ctrl + b, ?*. See how this time it just outputted a question mark rather than load the key binding help page, like it used to. This is because *Ctrl + b* has been returned to the underlying program, which, depending on the program, usually means "move back one character" and then *?* means "type a question mark."

Now the prefix key is *Ctrl + t*, so try it. Do *Ctrl + b, ?* and you should see the key binding help we saw before.

Rebinding the prefix key is a rather common operation, and this is the reason why throughout this book we have been using <Prefix> to denote it and not the actual key combination.

Most other keyboard combinations are usually left alone but many people have their reasons to favor another prefix key.

Binding keys without the prefix key

It is generally unadvisable to bind keys without the prefix key since this renders any key inoperable for all the programs running within tmux, but it is technically possible. It becomes inoperable because tmux will snag it and do the things tmux wants without passing that keystroke on to the program running within tmux. There are workarounds, such as binding <Prefix>, {key} to send the key through to the underlying program.

Say you wanted to bind the function keys *F1, F2, F3*, and so on to select windows 1, 2, 3, and so on, respectively. This would be possible by putting the following snippet into your .tmux.conf file:

```
bind-key -n F1 select-window -t :1
bind-key -n F2 select-window -t :2
bind-key -n F3 select-window -t :3
...and so on
```

Notice the -n option? This allows you to press the bound key without first pressing the prefix key. So you could simply press *F1* with no prefix and immediately switch to window 1!

This sounds like a really cool trick (and it generally is!), until you find even a single program that you want to run within tmux that expects the key *F1*. Then, since you've captured *F1* globally for tmux, it's not possible to use that keystroke within that or any other program because tmux captures it, uses it for the purpose you've specified, and never passes it along to the program. Again, you can use a trick such as binding <Prefix>, *F1* to send *F1* through to the underlying windows; however, for most users, it's probably not a great practice to get in the habit of globally overriding keys.

So, the most likely outcome here is that you can create some cool global shortcuts for something like that so they work for a while until you find an exception. You will then unbind them and end up having to convince your muscle memory to forget what it learned.

Unbinding keys

Now let's say there is a key binding that you want to remove for some reason. This is very easy; just add an unbind directive to your .tmux.conf file.

Say we wanted to unbind *0* from its default action of selecting window 0 for some reason. To do this, simply add the following code snippet to your configuration:

```
unbind 0
```

Note that there is no need to explicitly unbind a key before binding it to something else; every key can only have one binding. So, we find it rather rare to use this bit of utility, but it's nice to know it's there when you need it.

Status bar revisited

Last time we touched the status bar, we altered its colors, but we did not do anything to change its content. tmux allows us to change a lot of different aspects of the content of the status bar. We won't have an in-depth look at every possible configuration, but will explain the concept and show one example.

So, the status bar has three chunks basically:

- **status-left**: This represents the stuff on the status bar on the left-hand side, including the current session

- **List of open windows**: This appears in the middle by default
- **status-right**: This represents the stuff on the status bar on the right-hand side, including the current date

Recall our status bar, which appears as shown in the following screenshot:

```
[tutorial] 0:masterpiece- 1:~*                    "minerva.local" 21:39 30-Mar-14
```

By default, status-left shows the name of the current session in brackets. We named our session tutorial, so status-left for us is **[tutorial]**.

We can change these. They are just simple strings with some magic character pairs that tmux fills in based on what they mean. For example, one of the magic character pairs is #s, which tmux will replace with the name of the current session. So the actual value of status-left according to tmux is [#S].

tmux takes this magic character pair and replaces it with the name of the current session, and that's how we end up with **[tutorial]**.

The status-right string is similarly made up of these character pairs and can easily be replaced.

The following is a table with a list of all the possible character replacements. This comes verbatim out of the tmux man page:

Character pair	Replaced with
#(shell-command)	First line of the command's output
#[attributes]	Color or attribute change
#H	Hostname of the localhost
#F	Current window flag
#I	Current window index
#P	Current pane index
#S	Session name
#T	Current window title
#W	Current window name
##	A literal hash (#)

So let's say we wanted to change the value of status-left so it looks similar to {username@host} where the username and host are filled in automatically; we can easily do that. Simply add the following lines to .tmux.conf and reload the configuration (note that we also widened the status because the default is 10 and it was getting cut off):

```
set-option -g status-left-length 25
set-option -g status-left "{#(whoami)@#H}"
```

This will fill in the status bar with {victor@minerva.local} for me because it executes the whoami command, puts the output of that command into the string before @, and fills in the hostname after it.

Option types

Thus far, all of the options we have set had the -g flag. This means that the option applies globally. However, there are three types of options: server options, session options, and window options.

There are also multiple flags that indicate how a given option should affect or be affected. This sounds complex, but it's rather simple.

A server option will apply to any client that connects to tmux. Under the hood, when you type and run the tmux command the first time, tmux creates a server; then, it creates your client and connects to the server it started. This is the magic that allows you to detach your session, reattach it later, and have everything running as you left it because the tmux server keeps chugging in the background. So an option specified with the -s flag will apply to the server, meaning it will affect any clients that attach to it.

A session option will apply to the current session. This means that two clients could connect to the same server and each could have slightly different session options. This is in contrast with the server option, where every client has that same option whether they want it or not. Session options do not have a flag; they are set by leaving off the flag, as they are the default.

Then, there are window options, which apply only to one window. To set a window option, specify it with the -w flag.

When it comes to configuring options, they cascade down. So there are global options specified with -g that will serve as the master set. Then, any option further down the chain will inherit from the global settings or may override the global setting with its own.

There are a couple of other interesting flags. The -g flag as we've mentioned is the global flag, which means the option applies globally. Most of the time, when people set settings in tmux, they just use the -g flag because they have no need for more complex flags or settings.

The -a flag means that the option expects a string to append the supplied value with the existing setting. So, for example, if the existing setting for an option is banana, then a client trying to connect will append their own option with set-option -a " split", rather than override that option entirely. This will make the option banana split. This is often useful to append custom items to things such as status-left and status-right without clobbering the global setting.

The -u flag will unset an option, meaning that the session will inherit the option from the set of global options.

These option types and flags can be a bit confusing, but they provide a lot of power. Again, most people set options with the -g flag and call it a day.

Handy configuration tips

What follows are a handful of configuration tips we have picked up throughout the years that are a bit useful and not necessarily obvious even after understanding the mechanics of how to configure tmux. These tips include the following:

- Binding the double tapping of the prefix key to last-window
- Changing the escape time
- Lengthening the history limit
- Lengthening the display time
- Starting the base index at 1

Binding the double tapping of the prefix key to last-window

This is one of our favorite tricks. More often than not, once you switch to a window and see some information, you want to switch back to the one you came from.

As the title here implies, this can be made very easy by creating a key binding for the prefix key that performs the last-window command. This way you can double tap the prefix key to jump back and forth between two windows. Once as the prefix and once to run the last-window command.

To do this, simply add a `bind-key` entry to your `.tmux.conf` file and bind the same key combination as your prefix key to the `last-window` command. For example, if you followed the preceding steps and set the prefix key to *Ctrl* + *t*, the following line in your `.tmux.conf` file is appropriate:

```
# Double tapping the prefix jumps to last window
bind-key C-t last-window
```

Now moving on to the last window is as easy as holding down *Ctrl* and tapping *t* twice.

Changing the escape time

I have heard from some vim users that tmux adds a short, almost imperceptible delay between the commands that can cause funny behavior when running vim inside tmux.

In tmux terms, this delay is called `escape-time`. By default, it's set to 500 ms. To fix things with vim, set the `escape-time` to `0` by adding the following line to your configuration file:

```
set-option -s escape-time 0
```

Note that this option obviously exists for a reason, so tread carefully when doing this as you may come across unexpected behavior. However, we've heard from a lot of vi users that make this change and they never look back. Also note, as discussed previously, this has the `-s` flag so it is a session-specific option, which means that if someone else connects to the same server, they could have a different value for `escape-time`.

Lengthening the history limit

tmux only has a limited amount of scrollback history. The scrollback history is the number of lines it retains in memory that have scrolled off the screen and which are accessible in Copy mode (see *Chapter 4, Manipulating Text*).

However, the default `history-limit` for tmux is 2,000, which can be pretty low for many use cases. In order to crank it up, add the following line to your configuration file:

```
set-option -g history-limit 10000
```

Note that by increasing this history limit, you are also increasing the memory footprint of tmux. So some tweaking may be necessary if it's set too high, particularly if you tend to have a lot of open windows and panes.

Lengthening the display time

Some commands will cause tmux to display a message to you, replacing the status bar with the text it displays for you. The time a message is displayed is called `display-time`.

Out of the box, the value of `display-time` for tmux is rather low. Try doing a search for text in another window with some text that you know doesn't exist. For example, try <Prefix>, *f*, then type any search string that you know doesn't exist in any other window, for example, `potato`.

You will see the text `No windows matching: potato` appear in place of the status bar and then disappear in the blink of an eye:

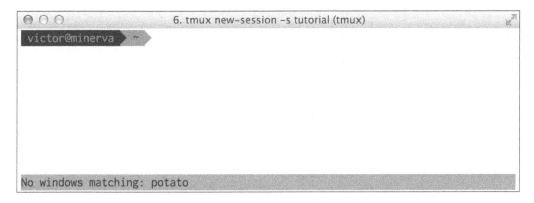

It will go in a flash because it only stays on the screen for the duration of the current `display-time`, which is only 750 ms by default. It's probably a good idea to crank the value of `display-time` up a bit so messages stay visible a bit longer, at least until you are more comfortable with tmux. To do so, add the following line to your configuration file, changing the duration to 2 seconds:

```
set-option -g display-time 2000
```

For a 2-second duration, we set `display-time` to 2000 because the display time is set in milliseconds.

Now is also a good time to note the `show-messages` command, which will bring up all the messages. It is accessible under the key combination <Prefix>, ~ and will show a nice list of all the messages that have been displayed:

```
●  ○  ○                   6. tmux new-session -s tutorial (tmux)
Sun Mar 30 20:50:41 2014 Window not found: :2                               [0/0]
Sun Mar 30 20:50:51 2014 Usage: rename-window [-t target-window] new-name
Sun Mar 30 21:27:49 2014 No windows matching: blah
Sun Mar 30 21:27:51 2014 No windows matching: blah
Sun Mar 30 21:29:36 2014 No windows matching: blah
Sun Mar 30 21:31:28 2014 No windows matching: potato
Sun Mar 30 21:32:54 2014 No windows matching: potato



[tutorial] 0:masterpiece- 1:~*                      "minerva.local" 21:39 30-Mar-14
```

This is very useful if you know a message was there but were not able to see it before it timed out and disappeared.

Starting the base index at 1

You probably noticed that, by default, tmux starts indexing the windows (and panes) with 0. The first window created is given the number 0, the second is given 1, the third 2, and so on.

This is not only a little confusing, but also makes the keyboard shortcuts for accessing windows a bit odd. To access the window furthest to the left, type <Prefix>, *0*, where *0* is the rightmost number key on the keyboard and then the second from the left <Prefix>, *1*, which is the leftmost number key on the keyboard, and so on.

This is easily avoided by changing what's called the `base-index` value. This `base-index` value determines the starting place so we can ensure it starts with 1 rather than 0. Note that we haven't discussed panes yet, but we will, and it also makes sense to set `pane-base-index` to `1` as well. So just trust us. Do it for now; we'll explain why later. Add the following to your configuration:

```
# Set the base-index to 1 rather than 0
set-option -g base-index 1
set-window-option -g pane-base-index 1
```

Note that if you already have a window 0, it won't go away. However, subsequent sessions will start without window 0, and if you remove window 0 from this session and create a new one, tmux will skip window 0.

Accessing the man page

For obvious reasons, we usually do not like to suggest going to the man page in this text as we try to explain most things in far greater detail than they do. However, when it comes to referring to an exhaustive list of options that can be configured in the .tmux.conf file, nothing really beats the man page.

To access, you can type the following command:

```
man tmux
```

> You can also access the man page on the Web at one of many resources that mirror the man pages online. The following is an example:
>
> http://man.cx/tmux

If you scroll down about halfway, there is a heading called **Options**. This contains the full list of options that could be set in our configuration file and a description of each one. Now that we understand how a bunch of them work, it should be much more manageable to view this man page and tinker with things!

Show options

If you find options in the man page, it may be useful to see what their current values are. Thankfully, this is easy!

Simply run the tmux show-options command with a flag for the set of options you want to view to look at the global options:

```
tmux show-options -g
```

For window options:

```
tmux show-options -w
```

For server options:

```
tmux show-options -s
```

You will see all the options printed out on the screen. This is nice to get a baseline or see the kinds of values that would be accepted.

Summary

So let's put it all together. Refer to the *Appendix* to see the final product, the `.tmux.conf` file we have built throughout this chapter.

Throughout this chapter, we learned a lot about configuring tmux. Starting with a blank `.tmux.conf` configuration file, we built up a much larger configuration changing many aspects of our tmux experience.

We altered the look and feel by modifying the status bar, and we learned how to bind keys, including the prefix key. We showed you how to bind multiple commands to a single key binding and how to unbind keys. We learned how to keep the file manageable and well documented by adding comments, and how to bind keys without needing the prefix key. We learned about the different types of options that can be set in the configuration file and some handy configuration tips that probably wouldn't be readily obvious to most readers.

By the end of the chapter, we have built up a very rich sample configuration file, which can be a great starting point for your own personal customization. We learned a bit about how to browse the man page for an extensive list of the available options.

We hope you treat this `.tmux.conf` file as a living document and update it with other neat things you may find and remove or change any bits that exist in it now. Personalize it to suit your needs; after all that's what it's for!

Now that we've learned all about configuration, in the next chapter, we will move on to discuss one of the major fundamentals of tmux: the concept of sessions, windows, and panes.

3

Sessions, Windows, and Panes

In the previous chapters, we discussed sessions, windows, and panes; now we are going to dive deeper to understand the differences between them and how they can help in maximizing your productivity.

In this chapter, we will cover the following topics:

- What sessions, windows, and panes are, and how they relate to each other
- How to create multiple sessions and switch between them
- How to create multiple panes
- Zooming panes
- Splitting and resizing panes
- Switching between panes
- Cycling through pane configurations

Overviews

First, let us have quick overviews of sessions, windows, and panes before we get into how they fit together. We have mentioned them lightly in different contexts now, but they are crucial to understanding tmux and are worthy of more exploration.

Sessions

We got a nice taste of sessions back in *Chapter 1, Jump Right In*, when we named our session `tutorial` and detached and reattached our session.

Sessions are essentially the base unit in tmux. It can have one or more windows, and a window can be broken into one or more panes.

It may be useful to think of a tmux session like the login process on your computer. Whether you have a computer that is running Windows, Linux, OS X, or Unix, they all support multiple simultaneous logins in some form.

When you log on to your computer, it initiates a new session. You type in your username and password and then hit *Enter*. You will then arrive at a nice, empty desktop. This is a session on your desktop computer. On this desktop session, you can run one or more programs, where each program has its own window or windows and each window its own state.

Likewise, tmux parallels this concept. When you initiate a new tmux session, you start with a nice and empty status bar. This is your session on tmux. In this session, you can create multiple windows, run a program in each window, and each window has its own state (this is a slight simplification, as we will soon see). When you switch from one window to the other, the state is maintained. That is, the things which you typed or entered, before switching from one window to another, are still there when you switch back to that window.

In most operating systems, there is a way for you to log out and log back in to arrive at the same session, with the windows and the state just as you left them. Often, some of the programs you had opened will continue to run in the background and even receive updates when you log out, even though their windows are no longer visible. With most operating systems, there is some concept of a window manager, so there is often much more running in the background than you can see at any given time. For instance, on an iPhone, Android, or other smartphone, only one program actively fills the screen, but others hum along in the background receiving mail messages, listening for incoming calls, playing music, and doing other background tasks.

Likewise, with tmux, you can initiate a session, open some windows, do some work, detach that session, and everything keeps running in the background as you had left it. We saw this back in *Chapter 1, Jump Right In*. You switched from an editor to another window, typed something, went back to the editor, and it was still humming along just as you had left it. You also detached a running session and reattached it later, and everything was still as you had left it. This is the power of sessions.

So, a session in tmux is like a little mini operating system that manages running programs, windows, and more, all within one or more sessions.

Thus far, we have only seen examples of having a single session open, but it's quite possible to have multiple sessions open simultaneously and easily switch between them. We will run through an example of this later in this chapter.

It is often easy and convenient to group tasks logically by sessions. Sessions can also be given names, as we saw when we named our session `tutorial` back in *Chapter 1, Jump Right In.* This way, you could logically group things into sessions having, for example, one session for one project and another for a different one.

Windows

Windows are the next building block. Each window is what fills up the terminal application. Think of it like a viewport or tab in your web browser.

By definition, only one window can be active and viewable at a given point in time in tmux. We created multiple windows in *Chapter 1, Jump Right In*, and showed you how to switch back and forth between them.

Each window gets an entry in the status line, much like each browser tab has a tab visible in your web browser.

By default, windows get their names from the programs that are running within them, but it's also possible to specify a name for each window.

Each window can be broken down into one or more panes.

Panes

It seems as though we haven't seen any panes yet, but we have. By default, each window starts with a single pane that takes up the whole window.

Thus far, we have only seen windows with a single pane, so it seems as though we have only seen windows; however, in reality, we have seen windows, each with a single pane that took up the whole window.

Things get really neat when we take all of these window panes and split them into smaller panes, each visible simultaneously. Say, you want unit tests and code linting running in two different panes, both visible at the same time so when your files are saved, they will not only run, but will also be visible—a perfect task for two panes!

We can take a pane and divide it into two or more smaller panes, each running different programs. These panes can be resized, and they can be zoomed to temporarily take up the entire window. These panes can be converted into a new window or even attached to other windows. This power and flexibility that panes provide is something most other programs do not.

A window and a pane are perfect analogies to their real-world counterparts. Check out the different physical, real-world windows, and you will find that many of them are nicely divided into multiple panes.

 One nice benefit of panes in tmux over panes in the real world is that they are easy to create, destroy, and resize based on your needs. You cannot do that with panes on most physical windows.

Playing around with sessions, windows, and panes

So now that we have a high-level understanding, let's take a little tour of sessions, windows, and panes. Let's start totally fresh with a new terminal window and no existing tmux sessions. Start by creating a session named **work**:

```
$ tmux new-session -s work
```

You'll see a new session started with the name **work**. This session, currently, has a single window with a single pane.

Let's create another window. Recall that this is done by pressing <Prefix>, *c* (*c* for create). Now you have one session, two windows, and two panes. Each window has a single pane, as shown in the following screenshot:

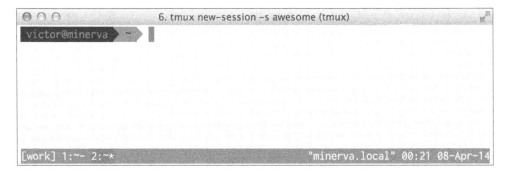

Multiple sessions

Now let's see what it's like working with more than one session. Let's first detach the current session. Recall that in order to do so, we'll press <Prefix>, *d* (*d* for detach).

Now that the **work** session is detached, we are back at a command line, and your screen should be similar to the next screenshot. Instead of reattaching the work session, let's create a new session and call this session **play**:

```
$ tmux new-session -s play
```

Now it looks like we have an entirely different session. We have a different status bar with the session name **[play]** in the bottom-left corner rather than **[work]**.

Now to switch back to the work session, we could detach the play session, arrive back at a tmux-less terminal and then reattach the session, this time with the work session as the target; however, there is actually an easier way.

Simply press <Prefix>, *s* (select the session interactively); this will bring up a dialog where we can take our pick about which session to attach. So, we didn't even need to leave the session we were in to switch to the other one. Use the arrow keys to highlight the session you want, or just tap the number associated with that session to switch.

Try switching to the other session, then back again, but wait, there is an even easier way. Simply use <Prefix>, *)* (next session) and <Prefix>, *(* (previous session) to cycle around between the sessions. You'll see it's very easy to switch between sessions. We'll skip switching between multiple windows since you already know how to do that from the first chapter; let's move right on to multiple panes.

Multiple panes

Now let's break this window into two panes. Type <Prefix>, % (split the window vertically) and see how the window is now divided down the middle by vertical bars; we now have another command prompt. This is the second pane, as can be seen in the following screenshot:

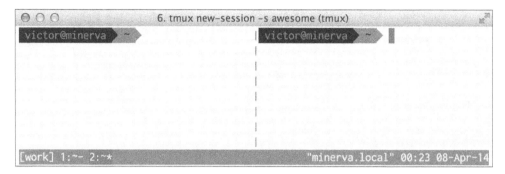

Now we have two sessions, three windows, and four panes. One session, one window, and one pane make up the play session (which is no longer visible but humming along in the background), while one session, two windows, and three panes make up the work session we saw in the previous screenshot.

Let's play around with panes a bit. First, try typing in some text. You'll see the cursor is in the right pane. To get it to the left pane, simply press <Prefix>, *o* (*o* for other). Now your cursor is in the other pane. Type some stuff to verify which pane the cursor is in.

There is actually a better way to tell which pane has the cursor than typing in random stuff. It may be tough to tell from the previous screenshot; however, when a window is split into two vertically, the top half of the vertical bars that split the two windows will be colored when the cursor is in the left pane, and the bottom half will be colored when the cursor is in the right pane. In the previous screenshot, the bottom half is colored in green to indicate that the cursor is in the right pane. When there are more than two panes, tmux tries different schemes to let us know which pane is active, as we soon shall see.

You can also use <Prefix> and the right arrow key, <Prefix> and the left arrow key, <Prefix> and the down arrow key, or <Prefix> and the up arrow key to move the cursor to the pane to the right, left, down, or up, which is a bit easier to remember and also more useful when we have a more complex pane structure.

Working with more panes

Now <Prefix>, % (split the pane vertically) is not the only way to create panes. This simply splits the current pane into two smaller ones by splitting it vertically. If you actually do it again, it'll split the current pane in half again with another vertical line, as shown in the following screenshot:

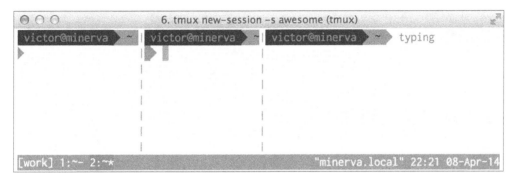

This is rather silly and scrunched though. First, let's kill that pane and then try to split it vertically. To kill the new pane we created, we can either terminate the running program in that pane, in this case, typing `exit` and pressing *Enter* as this will end the shell process. Alternatively, we can press <Prefix>, *x* (kill pane) to be prompted whether to kill that pane or not.

 Note that killing a pane with a running process will terminate that process immediately without gracefully ending it, so you will lose any existing data in that pane. Be careful!

Confirm with *y*, and you're back to two panes. Note that when a pane is removed, things are automatically resized appropriately. Let's try to split the left pane horizontally. In order to do this, type <Prefix>, " (split the pane horizontally), as shown in the following screenshot:

Now notice how the active pane is rimmed by green. This is the way tmux highlights the current pane with more splits, as we alluded to previously.

Now we've got a nice horizontal split in that left pane. Let's split that pane vertically just to show how pane-crazy we can get. Press <Prefix>, % (split the pane vertically) to split it vertically one more time, as shown in the following screenshot:

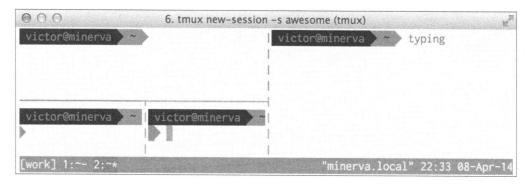

Zooming panes

OK! Now the panes are tiny and silly, but we can help them, temporarily at least, by zooming the current pane to fill up the entire window.

Type <Prefix>, z (zoom the pane), and you'll see the pane zoom to take up the entire window. If you look at the status bar for the current window, you will see a Z added after the asterisk (*) to indicate that the window is currently filled with a zoomed pane.

When you are done operating on this zoomed pane, the same command <Prefix>, z will zoom it out back to its normal place in the window.

Resizing panes

OK, now things are a bit silly here with all these panes. Let's try to resize them a little so things are a bit more manageable. First though, let's type some random text in each pane so we can tell them apart.

Have a look at the following screenshot where we have written **Apple**, **Banana**, **Cherry**, and **Date**. You can do so by typing in one window, then using the <Prefix> key followed by the arrow keys to move on to the next one until all panes have some unique text, as shown in the following screenshot:

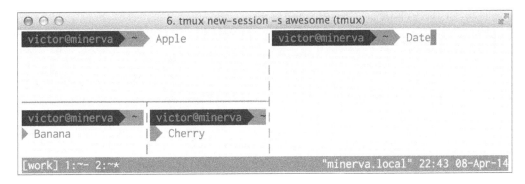

Let's try resizing the panes by some decent increments. Get the cursor over to the Date window, either using <Prefix>, arrow keys or <Prefix>, *0*.

Now to resize it, let's try <Prefix>, *Meta* and the right arrow key. You should see the rightmost pane get a bit smaller. Try it again and it gets even smaller. Try <Prefix>, *Meta* and the left arrow key, and you should see the rightmost pane get a bit larger.

> If you look at your keyboard and see no *Meta* key, you are not missing anything; it does not exist on most keyboards.
>
> *Meta* is a key often used in terminal programs that historically had a place on the keyboard, but no longer.
>
> Both iTerm and the stock terminal program on Mac have the choice to use the *Option* key as *Meta*. Other operating systems often have some way of using the *Alt* key as *Meta*.
>
> Though this may seem confusing, we use Meta in this book because that is the way it is referred to historically, and more importantly, because this is the key referred to in the tmux documentation.

Thankfully, you don't actually have to type the prefix key every time you want to resize it a little bit; as soon as you start resizing, you can just type the command to increase or decrease over and over without the prefix key. So start by using <Prefix>, *Meta* and the right arrow key, then you should be able to change the panes by holding down the *Meta* key and by pressing the left arrow key, the right arrow key, or the left arrow key. You will see the panes expand and contract without having to stop and type the prefix key each time.

This is one way to change the size of a pane. This is actually changing it in steps of five cells at a time (each cell being basically the space of one mono-spaced character).

It's also possible to be a bit fine-grained with it, changing the size in steps of one cell at a time. Simply press <Prefix>, *Ctrl* and the arrow key. However, this will move in much smaller increments and will also conflict with the command to switch between spaces on OS X.

If you have followed along with *Chapter 2, Configuring tmux,* and turned on the `mode-mouse` option along with the `mouse-select-pane` and `mouse-resize-pane` options, you can also use your mouse to select the active pane. You can do this by just clicking on the active pane and resizing the panes by clicking and dragging them on to the active pane. While this has the downside of reaching for your mouse, it can be the easiest way to rapidly arrive at a desired pane configuration.

Switching between panes by number

Now that we have so many panes, switching between them can get a bit unwieldy. The arrow keys are pretty nice but can still be a tad annoying. Thankfully, there is an easier way. Press <Prefix>, *q* and you will see a number appear in each pane and then disappear shortly thereafter.

The currently active pane will be of a different color than the other panes. This will also show the dimensions of each pane.

Just as each window was assigned a unique number, so also each pane is assigned with a unique number in every window. If you press <Prefix>, *q* again and, before the numbers disappear, type the number that appears in that pane, you'll automatically switch to it.

By default, the duration for these numbers to remain on the screen is 1 second, but you can change that by adding the following option to your `.tmux.conf` file:

```
set-option -g display-panes-time 3000
```

This will extend the time that the pane numbers are displayed on screen to 3000 ms or 3 seconds, allowing you more time to select a pane by its index.

So, to jump to the pane with the word Apple typed in it, simply press <Prefix>, *q,* and *1.* It does not matter which pane you were in previously since this pane is given an index of 1; using that key combo will jump to that pane.

Cycling through pane layouts

tmux provides us with a few different ways to change the pane layout automatically so you don't have to meticulously split and resize in odd ways to get to your desired result.

The most versatile of the bunch is a key binding that will essentially cycle through to a different preset pane layout each time you press a key combination. This key combination is <Prefix>, Space bar (cycle through pane layouts).

Try it out; press <Prefix>, Space bar, and you will see your panes move around. The content stays in them, so any programs in them would keep running fine, but they get rearranged and resized in different ways each time you use that key combination.

If you look at the status bar, you will see the name of the layout. There are five different preset layouts that you can cycle through; these are `even-horizontal`, `even-vertical`, `main-horizontal`, `main-vertical`, and `tiled`.

Until you know what you like for a given use case, cycling through them is a pretty good way to see what the possibilities are.

Once you are comfortable enough with these layouts, you can switch to them directly, without cycling through all of them, by pressing <Prefix>, then *Meta* and the index of the preset layout in the previous list. So, for example, you can use <Prefix>, *Meta + 1* to switch to the even-horizontal view, <Prefix>, *Meta + 2* to switch to the even-vertical view, and so on.

Other pane operations

There are far too many pane operations, so we'll not be able to cover all of them exhaustively in this book; for most that we'll not discuss, we implore you to dig into the tmux man page:

```
$ man tmux
```

Alternatively, you can refer to them on the Web at `http://man.cx/tmux`.

Now that you understand panes, the man page should be very manageable and understandable on the topic of panes.

You can do things like breaking one pane out into its own window; rotating the panes; swapping one pane with another; moving a pane to another window; and arranging all the panes horizontally, vertically, tiled, and much more.

There are many more commands to resize panes, many of which don't even have keyboard shortcuts because they're not used all that much. Of course, you could add your own, and if you read *Chapter 2, Configuring tmux*, you should have all the tools in your toolbox to do so.

Summary

In this chapter, we learned a lot about sessions, windows, and panes in tmux. We learned how each of these fit into the tmux hierarchy, and we played around with them to solidify some of the concepts. We created multiple sessions, split windows into multiple panes, moved them around, and learned different ways to switch the cursor from one pane to another.

In the next chapter, we will move on to text manipulation and learn about how we can scroll back through the window history, how we can copy text from the window history into a paste buffer, and how we can paste that content.

4
Manipulating Text

There are two important components of tmux that we are yet to discuss in more detail, namely, **Copy mode** and **paste buffers**.

Copy mode is a mode in tmux that we can switch to; it allows us to select the text that already appears on the screen and copy it. Also, it allows us to move our cursor anywhere on the screen, even to places that have moved off the screen.

When an item is copied from Copy mode, it ends up in the paste buffer. As its name implies, this is a buffer that exists to hold anything that is copied so it can be pasted later.

Here is a quick summary of the features we will cover in this chapter:

- Window history and how tmux handles text that has moved off screen
- Explaining the two tmux modes
    - Scrolling up through the Window history
    - Jumping by search or line
    - Copying text into the paste buffer
- Interacting with the paste buffer
    - Pasting the last copied item
    - Viewing the whole paste buffer stack
    - Choosing an item to paste interactively

By the end of this chapter, we will know all about working with text from within tmux.

Explaining the Window history

One thing you may have noticed in the previous chapters is that commands with too much text output appear to get cut off. You can see the tail end, but the rest seems to go above the window. If you try scrolling up, it will not work. What is going on here?

The start of a command is not lost forever. It still exists; it has simply scrolled off the screen.

In order to work its magic and keep everything in a single terminal window, tmux has to hide all of the text that won't fit in the currently viewed pane. It keeps all of this text stored in something called **Window history**.

Think of it like pages in a physical book. A book contains far more text than you can see at any given point in time, but to make it manageable, all of that text is on pages that aren't visible at the same time. The one page that is visible is the one you have opened.

Similarly, tmux maintains all of the text that didn't fit on the pane you are currently viewing and tucks it away in the Window history.

Now, of course, tmux doesn't need to stack its pages in a way that one is on top of the other, like with a traditional book. So, they're more laid out, one above the next, for as long as the history is configured.

The following illustration helps visualize it:

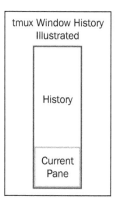

The diagram illustrates the entire Window history, most of which is not visible, followed by the contents of the current pane. Notice how the contents of the current pane are within the Window history. The Window history does not only contain contents that have gone off the screen, it also contains everything in the current pane.

By default, the Window history keeps 2000 lines, but as we saw in *Chapter 2, Configuring tmux*, we can increase or decrease this history to suit our needs as follows:

```
# Store more history in the buffer than default
set-option -g history-limit 10000
```

A larger history retains more of the state but also causes tmux to use more memory.

It is also possible to clear this history on demand with the tmux command, `clear-history`. You can run it by typing the following in a terminal:

```
$ tmux clear-history
```

Now it's nice that tmux stores all of that history for us, but it's useless unless we can do anything with it. Thankfully, we can access it with Copy mode.

Explaining the different tmux modes

tmux actually has a few different modes that can be used when interacting with it, such as Default mode and Copy mode. If you're a vi user, these modes are very similar to vi's insert and normal modes:

- **Default mode**: This is what we've seen thus far while interacting with tmux, which is mostly just giving us an interface atop the programs in the underlying window. This is similar to vi's insert mode. You are in Default mode by default, and if you go into any other mode and then exit it, you'll end up back in Default mode.

- **Copy mode**: This allows us to access the Window history and copy/paste contents from that history. It is similar to vi's normal mode in that it allows you to move around without tinkering with the underlying programs, just like vi's normal mode allows you to move around without altering the underlying document. It can be accessed by <Prefix>, [.

- **Command mode**: This mode is used to enter arbitrary tmux commands. It is similar to the vi mode of the same name and can be accessed by <Prefix>, :.

- **Clock mode**: This mode shows the current time and is more of a novelty/utility than an actual mode, like the rest. It can be accessed by <Prefix>, *t*.

- **Control mode**: This mode allows third-party applications to interact with tmux through a text-only protocol.

In addition, this is where we start to get to the text manipulation goodies within tmux. When we drop into Copy mode, we can scroll back to look back through the Window history, and we can also access some cool text manipulation tools.

Let's walk through a sample workflow with Copy mode.

A sample workflow with Copy mode workflow

If you have followed us from the beginning of the chapter, you should have a tmux session started. Let's first rerun the long-running command we used previously to list the available key bindings:

```
$ tmux list-keys
```

Just as we saw the last time we ran this command, only the last few lines are made visible in our current pane. However, now we are armed with a bit of knowledge about the Window history and can likely surmise that the remaining lines are there but have scrolled off the screen. How can we scroll up and see what that text was? Copy mode!

Entering Copy mode

Let's enter Copy mode so we can scroll back and see the rest of it, which is stored in our Window history. Press <Prefix>, *[* to switch back to Copy mode.

The first thing you'll notice is a new interface element added to our screen. There will be a new box in the upper-right corner of the terminal screen that shows **[0/76]**, as shown in the following screenshot:

This shows us both the number of lines in the history (**76**) and the current line our cursor is currently on (**0**).

Note that these lines are in reverse chronological order, so 0 stands for our currently viewed pane, 1 is a line above it, 2 is a line above line 1, and 76 is way up at the top of our Window history. This helps give context as to where in the history we are as we scroll up through it.

Going back to our Window history diagram, the lines can be thought of as shown in the following diagram:

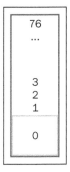

The first number in the **[0/76]** bit will show you the index of the lowest visible line on the current viewpoint. This can be a bit confusing at times as it seems, when you scroll up, that the first number doesn't start going up until you scroll your cursor past the current pane; however, it makes a bit more sense when you scroll down and bring the lines into the current view one by one.

Moving the cursor around

Now that you're in Copy mode, you can move the cursor up, down, left, or right, one character at a time. This is, rather intuitively, the up arrow, down arrow, left arrow, or right arrow keys or *Ctrl + p, Ctrl + n, Ctrl + b, Ctrl + f* (*k, j, h, l*). Try moving the cursor around a bit in Copy mode.

Emacs or vi style key bindings for Copy mode

Actually, there are two main ways to bind keys in tmux for Copy mode: Emacs-style key bindings or vi-style key bindings.

This is configurable using the mode-keys option. We will be primarily covering the default (Emacs-style) key bindings and will include the vi key binding in parenthesis following it. However, note that as we saw in *Chapter 1, Jump Right In*, tmux is smart and may alter the defaults based on your environment variables. So, while Emacs is the usual default, you may, without any configuration, be set to the vi mode with tmux out of the box, based on another configuration.

If you are a vi user, know that you can set up `vi-style` mode keys, and if you do, then the keys to browse Copy mode are very much like browsing vi's normal mode.

The Emacs key bindings for Copy mode can be viewed with the following command:

```
tmux list-keys -t emacs-copy
```

The vi key bindings for Copy mode can be viewed with the following command:

```
tmux list-keys -t vi-copy
```

Alternatively, you can look at the man pages under mode-keys for more details on configuring and which key does what (`http://man.cx/tmux` or man tmux from a terminal).

Now let's scroll up and see what's left behind.

Scrolling through the Window history

To scroll up a page, you can use *Page Up* or *Meta + v* (*Ctrl + b*) and you'll see that each time you press it, the number in the upper-right corner changes from **[0/76]** to match wherever you currently are.

You'll also notice that you will soon see the text that wasn't previously visible. That's right, now you're scrolling up into the Window history! Of course, you can also use *Page Down* or *Ctrl + v* (*Ctrl + f*) to navigate to a page back down.

You may find that *Meta + v* won't work to scroll up in tmux. If you encounter this, it is likely due to a configuration setting on your terminal.

If you are using iTerm2 on a Mac, you have the ability to specify how the terminal sends the *Option* key. To access this, visit **Preferences | Profiles | *Keys*** and you should see **Left option (⌥) key acts as:**. Set this to **+Esc** to have the *Option* key work like *Meta*, as shown in the following screenshot:

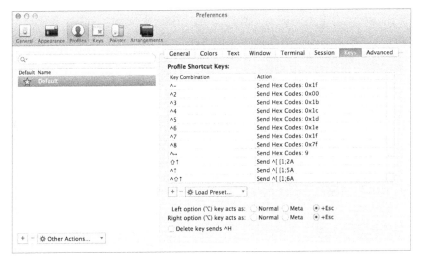

If you are using Terminal on a Mac, you have the ability to specify how the terminal sends the *Option* key. To access this, visit **Preferences | Profiles**, pick your active profile, select the **Keyboard** tab, and check the box that says **Use Option as Meta key**.

For other operating systems, *Alt* will often work as Meta out of the box.

You can also jump directly to the top of the Window history with *Meta + >* (*g*) and go back to the bottom with *Meta + <* (*G*).

Jump by search or line

Often, you know exactly what you're searching for when you go back through the history. When this is true, you can jump by a search term to get to a specific line.

For example, in Copy mode, press *Ctrl + r (?)*. You will see **Search Up:** appear in the lower-left corner, as shown in the following screenshot:

```
  ● ○ ○                    3. tmux new-session -s "Text" (tmux)
bind-key -r   M-Left  resize-pane -L 5                               [0/76]
bind-key -r  M-Right  resize-pane -R 5
bind-key -r     C-Up  resize-pane -U
bind-key -r   C-Down  resize-pane -D
bind-key -r   C-Left  resize-pane -L
bind-key -r  C-Right  resize-pane -R
Search Up: list-keys▶ █
[Text] 1:~* 2:..ments/writing-                  "minerva.local" 05:16 23-Apr-14
```

Type list-keys and then press *Enter*. You'll see you jumped directly to the last use of the term, list-keys, within the Window history. Try it again and you'll jump back to the time we first entered it.

If you don't have an exact search term, you can still jump directly to a line number. Simply press *g (:)* and you'll be prompted for the line to jump to. This is helpful when you don't know exactly what you may be searching for but would like to jump back several pages.

Leaving Copy mode

To drop out of Copy mode and go back to Default mode, simply tap *Esc* or *q* and you'll leave Copy mode.

There are many more keys to navigate to Copy mode, but it would be onerous to describe each one of them. However, we've seen most, and the rest is available on the tmux man page:

```
$ man tmux
```

Alternatively, you can find it with the tmux command list-keys -t emacs-copy or list-keys -t vi-copy, based on your chosen key bindings.

You can view more keys to navigate to Copy mode online at http://man.cx/tmux.

Copying text into the paste buffer

Now that we've gotten a taste of navigating around in Copy mode, let's put it to use.

Copy mode doesn't exist just to have a Window history that you can scroll through, but also to have a way to copy text from the past and reuse it.

Enter Copy mode by pressing <Prefix>, [and scroll around until you find some text that is of interest. Once you find something you'd like to copy, make sure the cursor is at the start of where you'd like to copy and press *Ctrl* + Space bar (Space bar). This sets the start point of the selection.

Now move the cursor around using the same keys as provided earlier, and you'll see the selection is highlighted and grows as you move away from the start of the selection. The area you select will have a different background color as the area is highlighted. See the following screenshot, which is an example of this:

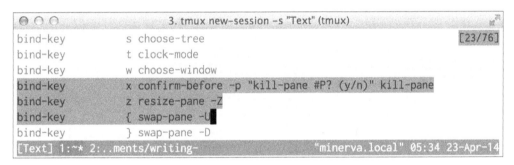

When you are satisfied with your selection, simply press *Meta* + *w* (*Enter*) to copy the text and you will leave Copy mode immediately and will be scrolled back to where you were. The text you selected will be copied and added to your paste buffer (more on this soon).

A few things to note are as follows:

- This is set up to model Emacs (or vi) almost identically in terms of key commands to navigate, copy, and so on. Things should feel rather familiar to you if you use Emacs or vi. If you aren't familiar with either, things may seem a bit foreign and will take some time getting used to.

- Note the copy operation is always nondestructive in tmux. You have copied the text out of the Window history but have not altered the Window history at all. So, you can go back and copy the same text again and again without disturbing the history.

- If you have tried copying text from multiple lines, you might have noticed the selection-wrapped lines. You can toggle it as a rectangle by pressing *R* (*v*) at any time in Copy mode before or after you start the selection. This is shown in the following screenshot:

- You can also grab all of the text to the right of your cursor or to the end of a single line of text, much like the kill line in Emacs, with the *Ctrl + k* keyboard command. Again, tmux's Copy mode is nondestructive, so this won't actually kill the line as it would in Emacs but will copy it to the paste buffer.

Interacting with the paste buffer

The paste buffer is a holding bucket for all of the text you will copy, which you will then be able to access later to paste onto any pane.

It is actually a stack, so each item copied from Copy mode is added at the top of the stack, and every new item is added at the top with every other item moved down by one. Each item in the paste buffer is assigned a number based on the order in which it went into the stack.

Pasting text from the paste buffer

Now that you've grabbed some text, you want to pull it from the paste buffer to get it back.

In any program that runs within tmux, move your cursor to the point where you want the text to be pasted and press <Prefix>, *]*.

For example, let's fire up nano:

```
$ nano
```

Once we do this, paste what we last copied with <Prefix>, *]*.

Sure enough, our text appears! Notice the nice symmetry, where you use <Prefix>, [to enter Copy mode, and <Prefix>,] to paste the text.

Now <Prefix>,] is nice to paste the most recently copied bit of text, but what about more complex situations such as copying two items and then pasting two items? Don't worry, tmux has it covered!

Choosing items from the paste buffer

The paste buffer is not just a single blob of text holding the last thing you copied; it is actually a stack of all the previously copied items. You can access this and paste from it in any order.

To access this list, simply press <Prefix>, =. This will bring up an interactive list of the last things you previously copied, as shown in the following screenshot, and you can simply highlight one and hit *Enter* to paste it:

By default, each time you copy it, it will be added to the paste buffer stack. Interestingly though, by default, when you pull an item out of the paste buffer, it will not pop the latest copied item out of the cache.

The command <Prefix>,] just quickly grabs and pastes from the top of the stack in (0).

Working with the paste buffer

There are also a handful of other useful things we can do when working with the paste buffer.

You can optionally set a limit for the number of items to store in this stack by setting the `buffer-limit` option to a number in your tmux configuration. This can be useful if you only want, say, the last five items you copied in a paste buffer for security reasons.

You can also list paste buffers non-interactively by pressing <Prefix>, : (list-buffers) and *Enter*, which will display all the buffers in a list that you can scroll through. Notice how each buffer has an index, which is a number, followed by the size of that buffer. Press *q* (*Esc*) to dismiss this list.

This buffer index can be used in a few different operations. It can be used to delete a buffer, to copy a buffer to another session, to load a buffer at a particular index, to set the contents in a particular buffer, to write a buffer to a file, and much more. It is a bit outside the scope of this book to cover all the things that can be done with buffers, but we will revisit a few very useful tasks in *Chapter 5, Diving Deeper*.

As in prior chapters, there is a full key binding and command reference in the appendix with all of the keys and commands we learned in this chapter handy, all in one place.

Summary

In this chapter, we learned a lot about manipulating text, starting from understanding the Window history to learning about the two different modes in tmux to scroll up through the Window history. We then moved on to jumping by search or line, copying text into a paste buffer, using Copy mode to copy text. We finished by discussing how to paste items from the paste buffer to the underlying window, how to view the whole paste buffer stack, and how to limit the number of items stored in the paste buffer.

In the next chapter, we will get to some more advanced usage topics, including a deeper understanding of the paste buffer, a bit more on sessions and windows, and an opportunity to get a taste of launching tmux with defaults.

5
Diving Deeper

Now that we have learned about text manipulation with Copy mode and paste buffers, we have discussed most of the basics of working with tmux. Let's dive deeper into some more advanced usage topics that could be helpful in your daily workflow.

We have gotten a taste of these items already, but this time around, we will explore them in more depth. In this chapter, we will cover the following topics:

- Understanding tmux commands and Command mode
- Advanced paste buffer usage
- Jumping from one window in a session to a window in another session
- Moving windows
- Linking a window between sessions
- Breaking panes
- Joining panes
- Launching a session with default windows

Understanding tmux commands and Command mode

You may have noticed that in prior chapters, we accessed some of our commands using different methods. For example, we showed you how to list the current key bindings. This can be done:

- By using the key combination <Prefix>, ?.
- By typing the command directly into a shell, prefacing the command with the `tmux` keyword, for example, `tmux list-keys`.

- By entering *Command mode* via <Prefix>, : and typing the command list-keys and then hitting *Enter*.

 Command mode in tmux is a lot like the mode of the same name in vi or the mode that we get by pressing *Meta + x* in Emacs. We touched on Command mode briefly in *Chapter 4, Manipulating Text*. Once you enter Command mode in tmux, you will have a prompt starting with a colon (:), and anything you type is entered into that prompt. Hitting *Enter* runs the tmux command you typed, like with vi.

What is going on here and why do all these three methods accomplish the same thing?

Under the hood, each tmux command is its own small program, much like the small classic programs underpinning any Linux, Unix, or OS X operating system such as ls, cd, mkdir, rm, and so on. You can actually view them all in the tmux source code online at http://sourceforge.net/p/tmux/tmux-code/ci/master/tree/.

Each of the commands is a small program, written in C and starting with the prefix cmd-.

When we type a key combination or run tmux command-name or <Prefix>, : command-name, we are instructing tmux to execute the code defined in that C file.

From here on, if we refer to a tmux command, keep in mind that it can be run using any of the three previously discussed methods.

Advanced paste buffer usage

We just covered paste buffers in the last chapter, but there is more than we were able to cover there. So let's cover some of the more advanced usage first while it's fresh in our memory. We'll touch on the following advanced paste buffer topics:

- Saving a paste buffer to a file
- Loading a paste buffer from a file
- Setting a paste buffer directly
- Capturing pane contents to a paste buffer
- Deleting copied text from a paste buffer
- Clearing the paste buffer history

Saving a paste buffer to a file

Assume you've just copied a lot of excellent text to the paste buffer and now you want to save it to a file.

Of course, you could open a text editor, paste the contents of the buffer, and save a new file; however, tmux provides us with a handy way to save a paste buffer directly to a file without all that fuss.

So jump back into your tmux session or start a new one and let's go!

1. First, find some text to copy. It could be any file with some text in it. For example, we have a sample file with some text that we print out via cat filename. You can use any file on your computer.

2. Recall that we can enter Copy mode by pressing <Prefix>, [.

3. Then, we can press *Ctrl* + Spacebar to start copying the text.

4. Move on to highlight the text.

5. Then, press *Ctrl* + *w* to copy it.

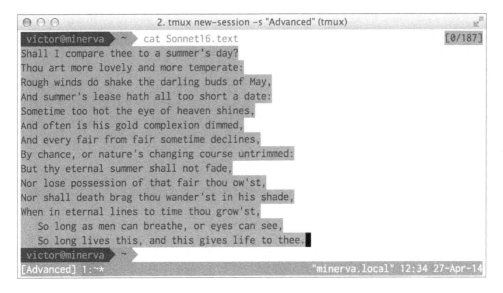

Alright, so now we have some text in the paste buffer at index 0. We can check this out with <Prefix>, =.

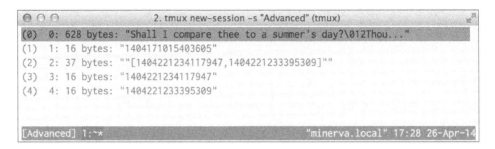

We have **628 bytes** there in that paste buffer. Hit *q* to dismiss that dialog. Now we can run the tmux command `save-buffer -b 0 [path]`; here, [path] is the location where we will save it and `-b 0` indicates that we want to save the text from the paste buffer with index 0, in this case, the text we just copied. After you run this command, we'll have a new file with the contents of that buffer.

So, for instance, <Prefix>, : `save-buffer -b 0 ~/sonnet16.poem` will save the contents of our paste buffer to a file. This can be extremely useful in many contexts. For instance, let's say you are using the `tail` utility to follow a log file in real time. If a useful snippet appears on the screen, jumping into Copy mode, copying it to a paste buffer, and then saving it to a file is a convenient way to copy the relevant text to a file. Alternatively, imagine you are reading a `man` file and want to snag a useful snippet to a file for later use. In this case, copying the snippet first and then writing that paste buffer directly to a file will store it for later use with expedience.

Loading a paste buffer from a file

We can also achieve the reverse, that is, loading the contents of a file into a paste buffer. To do this, simply run the tmux command `load-buffer [path]`, and the contents of that file will be loaded into a paste buffer.

This is very useful if you have text in a file that you want to paste into any program running within tmux; you can do this without having to navigate to and open that file in an editor, select all of the text in the file with the cursor, and then copy it in order to be able to paste it.

This can be incredibly useful, for example, as a way to utilize the core functionality of tmux to have a very powerful code snippet manager.

Say there are a bunch of different common boilerplate things you write in your code, such as a `for` loop, a function definition, or a class declaration. You could create a simple file for each snippet of boilerplate, load it directly into a paste buffer, and then paste it from within tmux. If you had a folder in your home directory called `~/snippets` and had boilerplate for a `for` loop with the name `~/snippets/forloop`, you could load it with the tmux command `load-buffer ~/snippets/forloop` and then simply paste it into the current buffer with <Prefix>,]. Over time, as you build up snippets for a lot of boilerplate code, you can save a lot of keystrokes.

By default, if no index is specified, the file's contents will be loaded into index 0, just as if you had copied it normally via <Prefix>, [(with each other paste buffer moving up one index); however, it's also possible to specify a buffer index to load it into.

Note that if a buffer index is specified, it must be an already existing buffer index, and it will overwrite the contents of that paste buffer with the index you will provide. So, for example, specifying buffer 0 with the tmux command `load-buffer -b 0 ~/snippets/forloop` will not end up in index 0, pushing all the buffers up by one; rather, it will entirely displace whatever was previously available in index 0.

Setting a paste buffer directly

It is also possible to set a buffer directly with tmux. This may be useful if you would like to paste the same text multiple times. There is no need to type the whole text out first and then copy it before being able to paste it; you can set the contents of a buffer directly.

For example, say we would like to put a sentence into a buffer directly. We can do this by issuing the tmux command `set-buffer`, optionally giving it an index and providing text to put into that buffer. The following steps will guide you in setting a paste buffer directly:

1. Try <Prefix>, :, `set-buffer "The quick brown fox jumped over the lazy dog"`.

2. Since we did not specify a buffer index, it will be pushed to the top of the stack, in buffer index 0, with the rest of the buffers moving down one index. We can view the contents of this buffer with the tmux command `show-buffer`. Sure enough, you'll see that the content is the sentence we just set.

3. Now paste it onto the screen using <Prefix>,].

Capturing pane contents in a paste buffer

With tmux, we can even capture an entire pane in a paste buffer. Use the tmux command `capture-pane` without any arguments to capture the contents of the current pane in a buffer. The output is shown in the following screenshot:

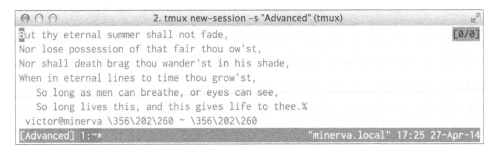

Then, view the contents of that buffer with the tmux command `show-buffer`.

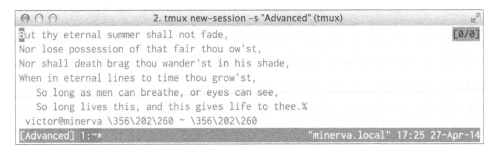

Note a few things:

- It will capture the contents of the current pane, but none of the tmux chrome. In other words, it won't include the tmux status bar or the **[0/0]** stuff in the upper-right corner that may have been present when you captured the pane.

- The `capture-pane` command will not always deal with the encoding of special characters, if you have any, present in the pane when captured, such as the ones you'll see in our previous screenshot. For example, see how the arrows and tilde for my command line came out as **\356\202\260**.

- It will capture the exact viewable portion of the pane so it knows how small or large your window is, and it will output exactly what's viewable in that pane at the current point in time only. (Note that it is possible to capture more than the pane that is visible, or less, by providing a start line index, end line index, or both to the `capture-pane` command.)

This command is very useful if you have a lot you'd like to copy and don't want the hassle of having to enter Copy mode and select the whole pane.

Deleting copied text from a paste buffer

Imagine you have copied some sensitive information using the methods we discussed. For most cases, it is very nice that tmux keeps it all around in the paste buffer stack, but what if you want or need to get rid of one or more items from that stack?

For example, say you used Copy mode of tmux to copy a password or a social security number; you probably don't want it sticking around forever in the paste buffer for someone to come along later and paste it. Thankfully, tmux provides us with the following ways to delete the text from the buffer stack:

- By default, the keyboard command <Prefix>, - will delete the last copied item from the paste buffer. This is the most convenient way to remove something you just copied/pasted. This has the side effect of bumping the index down of every other item in the paste buffer, like popping the top item off a stack.

- The tmux command `delete-buffer` will allow you to target a specific buffer and delete it. For example, `delete-buffer -b 2` will delete the buffer at index 2.

Clearing the paste buffer history

Similar to removing sensitive information from the paste buffer, you may desire to remove sensitive information from the tmux Window history, both on the screen and information that has scrolled off the screen.

This is particularly helpful if you use something like `pass`, a command-line password storage mechanism that will display your passwords on the screen when you retrieve them.

For more information, visit:

`http://www.zx2c4.com/projects/password-store/`

Once a password or some other sensitive information is displayed on the screen, it will seemingly remain in your Window history forever. This means that someone nefarious accessing your existing session may be able to just scroll back up through your history in Copy mode and see those passwords.

Running the Unix command clear within a pane will reset the viewport, but it does so simply by scrolling the other text up and out of the pane. If you move into Copy mode with <Prefix>, [, the contents of that window would still be visible once you scroll up.

Surely, there must be some way to purge that Window history to help prevent this. There sure is; it is the tmux command `clear-history`. Optionally, you can provide a target pane, and it will clear the history for that pane. For instance, `clear-history -t 1` will clear the history for pane 1 even if that is not your currently active pane.

While clearing the history, it will clear everything that was in the Window history that scrolled out of that pane, but it will retain everything that is currently visible in that pane. To clear the history and everything in that pane, it is best to run the Unix command `clear` first to push it off the screen, then the tmux command `clear-history` to flush everything.

Note that if there is extremely sensitive information that needs to be cleared, it may be best to restart tmux after you clear the Window history. This sensitive information, while expunged from the Window history and therefore not available in Copy mode, could still potentially be sniffed by a very capable hacker. Its bits may linger and be salvageable from a tmux memory dump, so restarting tmux is the only way to be entirely sure that it is gone from the memory as well. While this is a case that is quite on the fringe, it bears mentioning.

An advanced session and window usage

Back when we discussed sessions, we walked through how to switch from one session to another. What we didn't cover were some more advanced things such as switching from one window in one session directly to another specific window in another session, moving windows between sessions and sharing windows between sessions.

Jumping from one window in a session to another window in another session

A couple of chapters back, we discussed switching between multiple sessions using <Prefix>, *s* to bring up the list of sessions and select any of them.

OK! So let's get set up a bit. We'll need two active sessions with a couple of windows each. If you followed along the previous section, we should already have one active session; let's create another session using the tmux command, `new-session -s "Another"`.

Now let's create another window using <Prefix>, *c* and run some command in it, for instance, top:

```
$ top
```

The output of this command is shown in the following screenshot:

Let's switch back to our other session with <Prefix>, *s* and then highlight and select the other session we want, as shown here:

Jump onto the other session (**Advanced**, as shown in the preceding screenshot). Now if we do the same thing again, using <Prefix>, *s* and switch back to the **Another** session, we will arrive back in **Another**, in window 2 that is running top. This is because tmux will take us back to the last window we were viewing in an active session.

However, what if we wanted to move directly from one session to a specific window in another? Surely, we should not have to switch to the session and then select the window. Well, we can directly choose a window within a session, and tmux actually makes this a breeze.

Bring up the `choose-tree` interface again with <Prefix>, *s*. Notice the plus symbols to the left of the session names? They're there because that session can be expanded to show the windows running in those sessions. Simply highlight the session you want to drill into and tap the Space bar or right arrow key to unfold that session and see a list of the windows in that session. Notice how it resembles a file tree, as shown in the following screenshot. This is why this command has the name that it does.

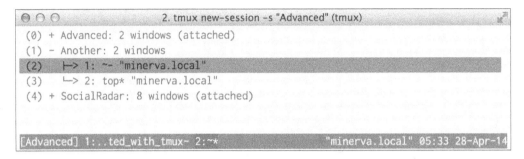

Recall from our first chapter what some of the magic characters on the window mean? The characters are as follows:

- The character * indicates the currently active window
- The character - indicates the previously active window

In the preceding screenshot, you can see that window **2** running **top** was our currently active window. If we just selected the session by choosing **(1)**, we would be plopped back into that session with the window running **top**. However, if we want to go directly to the other window, we can do this by highlighting it, refer to the previous screenshot, and hitting *Enter*.

Moving windows

So we've got **top** running in the session named **Another**. Imagine that we want to move that window to our session named **Advanced**. First, switch to the window with top running. Now run the tmux command `move-window`. It is conveniently bound to the keyboard shortcut <Prefix>, . so you can type that and then provide the name of the destination session which, in our case, is **Advanced**.

Note how that window is gone; now our **Another** session has only one window. The window with **top** was moved to the **Advanced** session, but we are still in the **Another** session. tmux opened the other window to keep us in the current session.

Now pull up the session list again using <Prefix>, *s* and then expand **Advanced**. In the following screenshot, we can see how it now has three windows, the last of which is the window that we just moved by running **top**:

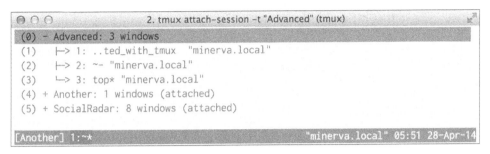

Note that this same command can also be used to move a window to a different index within the same session. We can specify the numerical index we'd like the window moved to within this session rather than providing a session name. For instance, to move a window to index 5, we could run the same move-window command via <Prefix>, . and then enter 5; by doing this, the status bar will be updated to reflect this window's new index.

When being moved from one session to another, the window will, by default, be placed at the lowest available base index. So, if you have set the base index to 1 and have windows in index 1 and 3, the moved window will land in this session with index 2.

To specify both the session and window index as the home for the window, specify both, separating them with a colon. For example, to move this window to the **Another** session in window index 7, you could use the move-window command with the argument Another:7 where the session comes before the colon and the window index after.

This is also useful to move a window to a session with a numeric name, such as the default session name *0*. By default, if you specify a number alone to the move-window command, tmux will assume you meant the window index 0 and not the session named 0. To specify this, you will use the command move-window 0: to explicitly specify the session named 0.

Linking a window between sessions

Now moving the window between sessions is quite useful, but what if we want to use the same program in multiple sessions and not have multiple instances of it running?

The `top` command is a great example. We could start another window now in our **Another** session which no longer has `top` because we moved it to **Advanced**, but then we will have two copies of `top` running; this will mean that we will be using double the amount of CPU and memory. There is nothing particularly interesting about `top` that will require us to have two instances of it running so doing so will be a waste of resources.

Therefore, let's not run two copies of `top` but instead link one window to both the sessions so it is accessible from either session.

First, let's open the window with `top` running. Now run the tmux command `link-window -t Another`. This tells tmux to link the window to the **Another** session as well.

You can use the same `session:window` syntax we saw previously for the `move-window` command to specify not only a destination session, but also a destination window index. For example, `link-window -t Another:5` will link this window to the **Another** session in window index 5.

The window is now accessible from both the sessions. In the following screenshot, it is window 3 on the **Advanced** session and window 2 on the **Another** session:

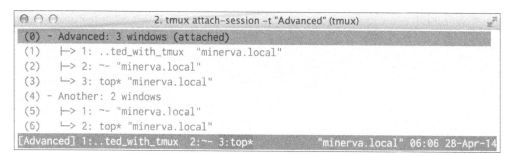

You can also link a window without first switching to it by specifying it as the source to the `link-window` command with the flag `-s`. For example, `link-window -s Advanced:3 -t Another:2` will link the window to the **Advanced** session, window index 3 to the **Another** session, window index 2 without requiring us to switch to the **Advanced** index 3 first as we did in the previous example.

So we are saving some resources by linking a window between sessions rather than creating a new one. This is useful for any command that does not require multiple instances to be effective that you may want accessible from multiple sessions. Aside from `top`, email clients such as `alpine` or `mutt` fall into this category, as do things such as `irssi` or a command-line music player. I will often run a window in the Org mode for Emacs linked like this so the list of to-dos is shared across sessions.

Note that if you do this, killing a pane or window in one place will kill it at both the places.

To later remove a window from one session but not the other, you will need to unlink the window rather than kill it by using the tmux command, `unlink-window`.

Breaking panes

The act of taking a pane within a window and moving it to its own window is called breaking that pane. It can be accomplished with the tmux command `break-pane` or the keys <Prefix>, *!*.

By default, the `break-pane` command will operate on the currently selected pane; however, any arbitrary pane can be specified using the same syntax we saw in the previous example to select a window within a session, specifically separating the session and window name by a colon. However, of course, a pane also has an index, which can be added after the window separated by a period. This all sounds complex, but it is actually rather intuitive.

For example, to select pane 2 in window 1 in the session **Advanced** and break it into its own window, we could use the command `break-pane -s Advanced:1.2`.

 Remember that you can see the current pane indexes flash on the screen briefly with the key binding <Prefix>, *q*.

When you break a pane, tmux automatically switches the window to select the window that now contains that pane.

Joining panes

In addition to linking windows between one session and another, you can also do something called joining panes. The name can seem a bit misleading at first, but essentially, this is used to take a pane in one window and move it to another window.

It can be used to move one pane in a multipaned window to another window, but it can also be used to take a window, which has only one pane, and join it with another (now its name is probably a bit less misleading). This is very useful if you have two windows running different things but decide you'd prefer them as two panes of the same window.

For example, let's say we have a pane running in one window and we want to join it with another window. In the simplest case, we could switch to the pane we want to join and run the command `join-pane -t :1` where `:1` indicates that we want the window in index 1 in the current session. After running this command, the window index 1 in the current session will have the contents of any panes it had before in addition to the new pane we just joined to it.

Using the same elaborate `session:window.pane` syntax we saw previously, we can specify a source pane and target destination to get really slick about it. Say we want to take the pane in the session **Advanced**, window 2, pane 1, and move it to the session **Another**, window 1, and not specify a pane number so it defaults to the lowest available index. We can do this with the command `join-pane -s Advanced:2.1 Another:1`

As you can now see, joining panes is an incredibly powerful tool in your tmux arsenal that will allow you to combine multiple panes into one. Now you have learned how to break a pane off into its own window, how to combine it with other panes, how to move windows and link them between sessions, and more.

Launching with defaults

Imagine you integrate tmux into your workflow such that you get very used to certain things being in certain places, perhaps a shell at the root of your code repository in window 1, Emacs in window 2, top in window 3, and so on. Now every time you reboot your machine, you spend some time to set up everything again, start a new session, create three windows, launch the programs in each window, and so on; there must be a better way. Of course there is!

tmux gives us some ways to configure things with nice defaults out of the box. We'll also see another way to do this later in *Chapter 7, Using Other Tools with tmux,* with a third-party utility.

So let's take the previous example and run through it. There are ways to make some of this happen within your `.tmux.conf`, file but it's generally more powerful to do it externally via a separate bash script. So hop into your favorite editor and start editing a new file named `.tmux.defaults`. You can name this file anything, so if you have multiple sessions you may want to name it based on the session name.

Now let's specify our configuration. In this file, copy the following code:

```
new -n term zsh
neww -n emacs emacs
neww -n htop htop
```

Of course, your commands may be slightly different based on your system configuration and what you would like to run by default.

Now, to run with this configuration file, start tmux as follows:

```
$ tmux source-file ~/.tmux.defaults
```

That's it! You'll see yourself get started in a new session with three windows: the first running a terminal, the second in Emacs, and the third in **top**.

Again, you can create multiple configurations like this by simply creating multiple files, one for each session you'd like to automate.

 For more details on launching tmux with defaults, check out the tmux manual section on session initialization: https://wiki. archlinux.org/index.php/Tmux#Session_initialization

It is possible to create more complex session initializations than our previous example, but complex configurations are often tasks better suited to third-party tools, as we will see in *Chapter 7, Using Other Tools with tmux*.

Summary

In this chapter, we revisited a handful of tmux topics, going into far more depth than we were able to in earlier chapters. At this point, you should have a great grasp and depth of information on paste buffers, sessions, windows, panes, and all of the other topics we covered in great depth here.

In the next chapter, we will not learn more about the mechanics of tmux itself, but rather a bunch of tricks and tips for its use that can help maximize your productivity.

6
tmux for SSH, Pair Programming, and More

By now, we have gone over nearly everything about the mechanics of tmux. Putting together everything from the previous chapters, we now know about configuration, sessions, windows and panes, text manipulation, and a smorgasbord of advanced usage in topics such as the paste buffer, moving windows, panes, and even launching sessions with some defaults. So at this point, we can use, configure, and customize tmux in many awesome ways.

Now, we will not explore new concepts in the mechanics of using tmux, but new ways to utilize the things we have already learned in order to simplify everyday workflows. In this chapter, we will cover the following topics:

- Using tmux over SSH for long lived sessions
  - ○ Setting up a virtual machine with Vagrant
  - ○ Workflow with tmux over SSH
  - ○ Launching tmux over SSH on connect

- Using tmux for pair programming
  - ○ Connection to the same session
  - ○ Using Vagrant Cloud for pair programming
  - ○ Using grouped sessions for pairing

Using tmux over SSH for long lived sessions

How many times have you been connected to a remote server over SSH just to have some network blip terminate your session, putting you back at square one when you reconnect?

With tmux, you can connect to a remote server, start a tmux session, and set up windows and panes the way you'd like them. Then, if you get disconnected from the remote server for any reason — be it a network blip, the SSH session timing out, disconnecting from a VPN, or simply closing your laptop to go home for the day — you can SSH into that machine later and reconnect to your tmux session which has continued running, preserving your state as you left it.

This is my favorite use of tmux and one that saves the most time in my daily workflow. Not only because it is useful to deal with network connectivity issues gracefully, but also since most remote servers running Linux are rarely terminated; this means that once you start a tmux session, it can persist for weeks or months.

Practically speaking, this means that every day when you connect to some remote server, you could be saving time setting everything up by using tmux. You won't have to change to the directory you usually want open in one window, you won't have to connect tail to a logfile in another window, and you won't have to open a file for editing in your favorite text editor in another. They'll already be there, just the way you left them before — thanks to tmux.

Let's walk through a hands-on example of this in action. For this, either connect to a remote server over SSH, or we have short instructions on using Vagrant to create a virtual machine locally to which you can connect.

Benefits of using Vagrant

Vagrant is an incredibly easy way to use virtualization to get a machine up and running locally. We suggest using it here for consistency.

The instructions we give *should* work when connected to just about any Linux server, but since there are so many different Linux distributions, versions, and more, there are bound to be slight inconsistencies.

By using Vagrant, we can ensure that the environment we authors have locally matches the instructions we provide which will match the environment you readers have locally if you also use Vagrant to set up your environment.

Having Vagrant set up will also prove helpful later in this chapter when we discuss using tmux for pair programming, which could open security vulnerabilities without a sandboxed instance like this.

If you would still like to skip Vagrant and just connect to a local machine, simply skip the next section and you should be able to continue with your remote box instead. Again, be forewarned that without Vagrant, some of these commands may not work exactly as specified and may need tweaking based on your Linux distro.

Creating a virtual machine with Vagrant

Ok, so we are going to create a virtual machine with Vagrant and we will then connect to it via SSH to illustrate some of the topics we will discuss relating to SSH. This will help give some consistency to the instructions and allow you, even if you have no access to a Linux server, to follow along.

First, install Vagrant. Instructions are available on the Vagrant website at:

http://docs.vagrantup.com/v2/installation/index.html

Next, navigate to a directory in which you'd like the Vagrantfile to live. A Vagrantfile specifies what should be installed when this machine is brought to life and its file can go basically anywhere.

So jump into your terminal and navigate to and/or create a directory for this file to call home. Now let's create a Vagrantfile. In a terminal, in your directory of choice, run the following command:

```
$ vagrant init ubuntu/trusty64
```

This will create a file in that directory named Vagrantfile. If you inspect that file, you will see it's rather simple with most of it commented out. We can leave most of the content in the file alone, but one bit we want to uncomment is the highlighted portion of the following snippet:

```
# Create a private network, which allows host-only
  access to the machine
# using a specific IP.
# config.vm.network "private_network", ip: "192.168.33.10"
```

To uncomment it, remove the # at the start of that line. It was line 26 in our Vagrantfile. This one change will ensure that we can connect to our machine locally via the IP address 192.168.33.10.

Next, let's add one line, directly after that line we just uncommented so that bit of the file should now look like the following code snippet:

```
# Create a private network, which allows host-only
  access to the machine
# using a specific IP.
config.vm.network "private_network", ip: "192.168.33.10"
config.vm.hostname = "tmux.dev"
```

This snippet is added so that we can SSH into our Vagrant box just as though it was our remote server in the cloud, and we can do so using the hostname tmux.dev.

> This hostname trick may not work depending on your version of Vagrant and your OS. If later, the machine seems inaccessible at the previous hostname, you can still access the Vagrant box at its IP address.

If we skip this, Vagrant does give us a way to connect to the box over SSH without needing the IP address (vagrant ssh), but then it will not look/feel like a remote server which is the intent here. So, although we'll be creating a machine locally, pretend it's the cloud server you connect to in doing your job. Let's start our virtual machine. Thanks to Vagrant, this is as easy as using the following command:

```
$ vagrant up
```

Now, the first time you run this, it'll take a little while. How long it takes will depend on the speed of your Internet connection, but for us it took about 7 minutes. It takes so long because it is downloading an image of an entire virtual machine with the latest version of Ubuntu.

Vagrant will give you some helpful output about what it's doing and near the end will ask for your password. This is your local user password and necessary because it asks for permission to write to your /etc/hosts file to add the entry to the name we provided (in our case, tmux.dev).

After Vagrant works its magic, we can connect to it. Make sure you detach your current tmux session if you have one active and run the following command line from a shell (not within tmux). If you run it from within tmux, you will end up with nested tmux sessions, which will be rather troublesome. From your command line, run the following command:

```
$ ssh -i ~/.vagrant.d/insecure_private_key vagrant@tmux.dev
```

Let's break this command line down a bit.

The `-i ~/.vagrant.d/insecure_private_key` part of the command specifies that we connect using this private key. This is the default created by Vagrant for this box. You can modify it to use your own personal private key but that's beyond the scope here.

The `vagrant@tmux.dev` part of the command specifies that we want to connect to the hostname we created, `tmux.dev`, and we want to connect as the `vagrant` user; the default user Vagrant creates when it initializes the box.

When you run this command you should be connected by SSH to our Vagrant machine!

Walking through a sample workflow with tmux over SSH

Let's now walk through our workflow with tmux over SSH. Thankfully, Trusty Tahr, the Ubuntu version we installed via Vagrant, comes with tmux already installed so we are ready to rock.

If you followed along and created a Vagrant box, you should have an SSH session connected to that machine. If you skipped the last session, SSH into your server and ensure you have tmux installed. Now, from your terminal on your SSH session in either Vagrant or a remote server, let's run the following familiar command to initiate a new tmux session:

```
$ tmux new-session -s MyServer
```

This command will launch a new tmux session called MyServer.

Now, let's do some stuff. Since every user has different needs and different workflows, we have a sample workflow we'll run through; as we run through the workflow, imagine substituting these steps for those which apply to your specific use. First, create a new window using the keyboard command <Prefix>, *c*.

One thing you may notice is that if you followed along earlier with *Chapter 2, Configuring tmux*, or if you created your own prefix key, it no longer works. Why is this?

You have created a brand new machine with Vagrant (or connected to a server). This is not your local machine. tmux pulls its configuration from the file ~/.tmux.conf, which does not exist on this other machine!

You can copy the file onto this machine (using the command $ scp -i ~/.vagrant.d/insecure_private_key ~/.tmux.conf vagrant@tmux.dev:~), create a new .tmux.conf file on that machine, or create a repository on GitHub with this (and possibly other dotfiles) that can be cloned on any remote machine you touch.

In this new window, open a file for editing using the following command:

```
$ nano myfile
```

Now create another window using <Prefix>, *c* and let's run **top**:

```
$ top
```

Open one more window by pressing <Prefix> *c* and let's tail a logfile this time:

```
$ tail -f /var/log/boot.log
```

Note that this is a rather boring logfile to tail as it won't change until next boot, but pretend it's an exciting web server logfile or something.

Ok, so now we've got four windows as shown in the following screenshot, each running different things on this remote machine using tmux:

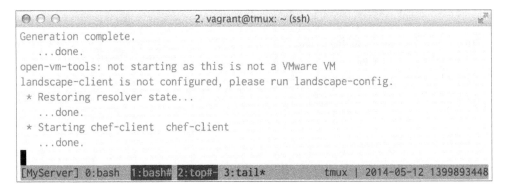

Now close your terminal window. Yes, I'm serious, trust me—everything will keep running! Imagine this is the same as dropping your network connection, having an SSH timeout, or going home for the day. Open a brand new terminal window. Run the following SSH command we ran before:

```
$ ssh -i ~/.vagrant.d/insecure_private_key vagrant@tmux.dev
```

Once you're connected via SSH, run the following command:

```
$ tmux attach-session -t MyServer
```

You can even run the following abbreviated version of the command to attach the session that you had running:

```
$ tmux attach
```

Lo and behold, there is everything just as you had left it! It will persist through all your disconnections for as long as that server stays up. Imagine the daily time saving in not having to open all these windows every morning when you connect to the server or any time you get disconnected!

Launching tmux on SSH connect automatically

You can also trigger tmux to be run on SSH connect automatically so you don't have to connect then start tmux. Close your terminal window again and open a new one. In this new window, run the following command:

```
$ ssh -i ~/.vagrant.d/insecure_private_key vagrant@tmux.dev  -t -- 'tmux
attach-session -t "MyServer"'
```

This tells SSH that after you connect, you want to immediately run the tmux `attach-session` command and reattach the session you had before. Now this is handy, but your command to connect to your server is getting rather long! We could place this long command in an executable shell script and run that script to connect to your remote server. Alternatively, we can also make things a bit easier by tucking most of it away in our SSH configuration. Jump into your favorite editor and edit the `~/.ssh/config` file. This file probably already exists; it is used whenever you connect to a server using SSH. Add the following lines to the file:

```
Host tmux
  HostName tmux.dev
  User vagrant
  IdentityFile ~/.vagrant.d/insecure_private_key
```

Now you can connect more easily with the following simplified command:

```
$ ssh tmux -t -- 'tmux attach-session -t MyServer'
```

Unfortunately, there is not a great way to tuck away the tmux command into the ~/.ssh/config file. There is, however, a way to do it on the server by tweaking the ~/.ssh/authorized_keys file.

We leave this as an exercise for the user as this is going in-depth into the concept and because it's not always desirable to initiate tmux every single time you connect to a remote host.

It could also create issues connecting to the remote host. For example, imagine you specify that on connecting the remote session should always run tmux attach-session -t MyServer. However, what happens when the session MyServer doesn't already exist? You could be locked out of the server! So tread carefully here dear reader.

Using tmux for pair programming

So we saw how to create sessions and how you can attach an existing session, but did you wonder what would happen if more than one terminal attached to the same session?

The ability to connect multiple terminals to the same session ends up being one of the biggest advantages tmux offers. By allowing two or more terminal windows to connect to the same tmux session, tmux becomes an extremely powerful collaboration tool. With tmux, two or more people can see and even interact with the same content at the same time!

Connecting to the same session locally

Before we get to full pair programming, let's try just connecting to the same session locally in two different terminal windows and see what happens.

If you followed the previous instructions, you should be able to pull up your tmux session by opening a new terminal window and running:

```
$ ssh tmux -t -- 'tmux attach-session -t MyServer'
```

That will connect to the box over SSH and attach your tmux session. Now, open another terminal window and run that exact same command again in this new window. You should notice that it is connecting and the session is looking very familiar.

Notice what happens if you type something in one window; it appears immediately in the other window! Now type in the other and you'll see the same happens in reverse. What you're seeing is the magic of tmux in all its glory. Each character entered in one window is propagated to the other and vice versa. You could even open up a third and you'd see the same behavior — typing in any of them also occurs immediately in the others.

Try switching from one window to another within tmux with the keyboard command <Prefix>, *n*. See how it changes in all windows simultaneously? How cool is that? Now you should be starting to see how this could be useful for pair programming. You could have one person in one place connected to a machine and someone else far away connected to the same machine and one person would see the other coding in real time and be able to interact as well!

Now try resizing one of the windows. Make it a bit wider and taller than the other window. Notice how there are dots along the edge in the larger window as shown in the following screenshot:

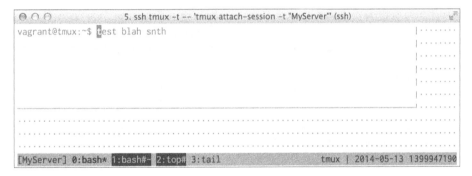

These dots are used as padding to ensure that the usable window size is the same for both viewers, regardless of the size of their terminal windows. This ensures the window within the dots will always be the size of the minimum height or width across all windows. This ensures consistency in terms of what each viewer sees, how each cursor moves, and so on.

This behavior can also be modified slightly with a setting called `aggressive-resize`.

What we described in this section is the default behavior, but this kind of resizing with dots may be unnecessary in certain circumstances — particularly if attached clients are not both looking at the same window at the same time.

The behavior can be modified to only pad with dots, as we have seen, when another client with a smaller window is currently looking at it. This helps constrain the resizing and letterboxing to only the case where it is likely useful. To enable `aggressive-resize`, put the following snippet in your `.tmux.conf` file:

```
set-option -w aggressive-resize on
```

Vagrant Cloud for better security pair programming

Now you may have seen the preceding example and noticed that in our example we both SSH'd into the same box as the same user. Unless you want to give your password or worse your private key to your pair, this is not a very workable solution. Your company may have a central server you both can access with your own accounts, in which case this may not be an issue for you. Otherwise, you may see this solution as a massive security hole. Even if you do have a shared server space, whichever of the pair is the "host" will open up their machine for shared viewing, which could be dangerous. If the other in the pair decided to copy the host's private key on a company server, there could be trouble.

This is why we suggest Vagrant Cloud for better security when pair programming. By spinning up a fresh virtual machine in the cloud, there is unlikely to be sensitive information accessible. You can share it at will with someone, trusted or not, and have a bit more piece of mind about security.

I have actually done this and used the pair programming for the coding part of a job interview on more than one occasion. You certainly wouldn't want to do that with an internal company server! If you'd prefer not to deal with Vagrant, simply jump to the next section.

So let's get started. The following steps will guide you in using Vagrant:

1. Go to `https://vagrantcloud.com/` and sign up. It's free to create an account.

2. Next, go back to a terminal, one not in the SSH session already (you can open a new one or detach one of the existing tmux sessions with the keyboard command <Prefix>, *d*), and enter the following command:

   ```
   $ vagrant login
   ```

3. Provide your username and password and you'll be logged in.

4. Navigate back to the directory where you created your `Vagrantfile` and run the command:

   ```
   $ vagrant share --ssh
   ```

5. You will be prompted to provide a password to encrypt the SSH key. Give it something that is a decent password but which you can share with the person you're pairing with.

6. On the screen, Vagrant will give instructions for the other user to connect and issue your machine a random name. Your current screen will look similar to the following screenshot:

```
                        4. vagrant share --ssh (bash)
aster  vagrant share --ssh
==> default: Detecting network information for machine...
    default: Local machine address: 192.168.33.10
    default: An HTTP port couldn't be detected! Since SSH is enabled, this is
    default: not an error. If you want to share both SSH and HTTP, please set
    default: an HTTP port with `--http`.
    default:
    default: Local HTTP port: disabled
    default: Local HTTPS port: disabled
    default: SSH Port: 22
==> default: Generating new SSH key...
    default: Please enter a password to encrypt the key:
    default: Repeat the password to confirm:
    default: Inserting generated SSH key into machine...
==> default: Checking authentication and authorization...
==> default: Creating Vagrant Share session...
    default: Share will be at: greedy-lamb-6478
==> default: Your Vagrant Share is running! Name: greedy-lamb-6478
==> default:
==> default: You're sharing with SSH access. This means that another user
==> default: simply has to run `vagrant connect --ssh greedy-lamb-6478`
==> default: to SSH to your Vagrant machine.
==> default:
==> default: Because you encrypted your SSH private key with a password,
==> default: the other user will be prompted for this password when they
==> default: run `vagrant connect --ssh`. Please share this password with them
==> default: in some secure way.
```

7. Now open another terminal window (simulating another user on a remote machine) and run the command it suggested. In my case, the command used was:

```
$ vagrant connect --ssh greedy-lamb-6478
```

However, the machine name will be different for you since it's randomized. After entering the SSH key password, you'll be connected via SSH to the server! This could be a person on the other side of the world.

8. Now run tmux and attach the session of interest:

```
$ tmux attach-session -t MyServer
```

And you're ready to rock.

Of course, the other person connecting will also have to sign up for Vagrant Cloud in order to connect. This is an incredibly easy way to come up with a relatively safe pair programming environment so two (or more) people can collaborate in real time over the Web without fear of compromising one of the collaborator's environments.

If the worst happens and one of the pair is nefarious, the worst they can do is make a mess of this virtual machine, which was created with only a handful of commands.

Using grouped sessions for pairing

You may have seen the previous pairing and thought, "Well that's great and seeing what the other person sees in real time is cool, but what if you want each person to be able to have different windows?"

This is where grouped sessions come in. You can have one person create a session and the next to join create a new session, but specify the grouped session as well. This way, each person has their own control over the windows in a session, but anything they do in each session is shared. This allows one person to be in one window and the other in another.

They can switch to each other's sessions at will, but otherwise don't need every command and keystroke to enact on both windows. To create a grouped session, one person must initiate the session as we discussed previously. If you still have the MyServer session running, you can use that.

In a new terminal window, connect to the same server but instead of attaching that same session with tmux, run the following command:

```
$ tmux new-session -t MyServer -s MySession
```

This instructs tmux to create a new session, but with the same target. This initializes a grouped session. The `MyServer` session is the grouped session, so the new connector can view it, but new connector can also switch to another window without stealing the initial user's view.

While this new session shares the same target, it essentially clones the original session and creates another for the second viewer. They are linked; so as one user opens new windows or changes anything in one session, the same will happen in the other session, but both sessions can have different names and both sessions will appear in the list of sessions as two different sessions. This way, if the second viewer kills their session (with the tmux command `kill-session -t {session name}`), the first session will continue running.

This allows the second user that connected to go off and do their own thing, creating more windows, using a different program, and so on, but without stealing the spotlight and forcing the host to watch their every move.

Now in each of our examples, we only showed two clients connecting to the same session. However, that could just as easily be 3, 13, 37, 359, or more. While there is no stated limit to the number of clients that can connect to a session simultaneously, there will be a practical limit on throughput and bandwidth and memory at some point. However, tmux does not enforce a set limit.

Summary

We learned some tricks of using tmux in a daily workflow. We learned how it can be used to help created long-lived SSH sessions and how it can be used for pair programming with a stop along the way to learn about using Vagrant to set up a shareable virtual machine.

In the next chapter, our last, we will discuss how we can use some other third-party tools with tmux to make it even more powerful.

7
Using Other Tools with tmux

As we saw in the past chapter, tmux is great for long lived SSH sessions and for pair programming with its own core functionality. However, as much as tmux is a fantastic development tool on its own, there are still some bits of functionality that it lacks. For example, as we saw back in *Chapter 5*, *Diving Deeper*, starting a tmux session with defaults is a bit difficult.

Thankfully, like many open source applications, there are many third-party tools that have sprung up to help fill those gaps.

In this last chapter, we will explore some of the best tools to augment tmux and make the tmux experience even more awesome. We will touch on the following topics/tools:

- Using tmux with the OS X Pasteboard
- tmux configuration from the maximum-awesome project, by Square
- Using tmuxinator to make session management easier
- Using wemux to ease the multiuser experience

Using tmux with the OS X Pasteboard

As the title implies, this first section is a Mac specific one. If you're on any other platform, skip it.

If you're used to the OS X Pasteboard and the command line, you may be familiar with the `pbcopy` and `pbpaste` tools. These are two small command line utility programs that ship with OS X that allow you to pipe command line content to the system-wide clipboard and vice versa.

A sample usage would be to run a command like the following:

```
$ cat Sonnet16.text | pbcopy
```

This command will print out the contents of the Sonnet16.text file and pipe them into the pbcopy program, which will then make the contents of that file easy to be pasted in OS X in any program with simply ⌘ + *v*.

The problem is that if you try this trick within a tmux session, it won't work! This is because the OS X Pasteboard doesn't play nicely. A short way to explain it is that because tmux runs its server as a daemon (which is what allows you to detach then reattach with it still running), OS X denies permission for it to access the Pasteboard. This is done for security purposes, so other programs running in the background are unable to access the Pasteboard. However, programs we'd like to have access to the Pasteboard, such as tmux, cannot access it without some tricks.

For the more information, see this lengthy description in **README** for a utility that fixes the issue: https://github.com/ChrisJohnsen/tmux-MacOSX-pasteboard#mac-os-x-pasteboard-access-under-tmux-and-screen.

However, since we do want tmux to have access to the OS X Pasteboard, surely there must be some way around this security restriction! Thankfully, some smart minds have come before us and solved the problem.

It'll take two steps. First, we'll install the small utility program. Second, we'll update our .tmux.conf file to launch every new window using this utility.

Let's first install the program. If you are a developer, you may already have Homebrew or MacPorts installed. (If not, we recommend that you install Homebrew: http://brew.sh)

Now, use the following command to install this utility using Homebrew:

```
$ brew install reattach-to-user-namespace
```

You can even use the following command if you prefer MacPorts:

```
$ port install tmux-pasteboard
```

Now, add the following lines to your .tmux.conf file:

```
# Make tmux and OS X Pasteboard play nicely
set-option -g default-command "reattach-to-user-namespace -l zsh"
```

Here, zsh can be replaced by your shell of choice, so it could be bash, or fish, or any other shell of your choice. By adding these lines to your configuration, you are basically telling tmux that any new window it launches should launch with that command rather than just a normal new shell. This new command is a shell that has been patched to play nicely with the OS X Pasteboard so pbcopy and pbpaste work as intended.

You may notice that this will only work on a system with the reattach-to-user-namespace utility installed and will cause issues on Linux or another Mac that did not have that installed. This can be remedied by using the following formulation instead:

```
if-shell 'test -x /usr/local/bin/reattach-to-user-namespace' 'set-
option -g default-command "reattach-to-user-namespace -l zsh"'
```

This will run only on systems that have this reattach-to-user-namespace command. The if-shell bit is a very useful little tmux command that will run the second command that follows it, provided the first command that follows it returns success. In our case, using the test -x command allows us to check and see whether the reattach-to-user-namespace file exists. If it does, it runs the tmux set-option to use the fixed item. If not, it runs nothing, so it will not break on systems that do not have this script.

tmux configuration from the maximum-awesome project, by Square

While we're on the topic of configuration, we should discuss the maximum-awesome project, and the configuration files for Vim and tmux from the folks at Square. Square specializes in payments and is very active in the open source community.

They have put a ton of thought and effort over the years into curating what they consider to be the ideal configuration for Vim and tmux and they have it freely available on GitHub: https://github.com/square/maximum-awesome.

Be forewarned, their configuration is rather Vim opinionated, but that caveat aside, they have baked up a truly awesome set of configurations.

Our favorite thing about these configuration files is that they provide a good set of defaults and recently added support for a .tmux.conf.local file intended for user overrides and custom commands. They are both great drop-in configuration files and great sources of inspiration for creating your own configuration.

So let's give maximum-awesome a go. Navigate to a directory where you can clone this repository. For example, we'll do it in our home directory. Enter the following command to get started:

```
$ cd
```

Then, clone the repository with the following command:

```
$ git clone https://github.com/square/maximum-awesome.git
```

Next, change into that directory:

```
$ cd maximum-awesome
```

Run the `rake` command to install the project:

```
$ rake
```

 Here, `rake` is short for the Ruby command `make` and it is the ruby analogue to make. If you do not have it installed, it can be installed with the command `gem install rake`. If you do not have gem installed, look to the RubyGems website for instructions: `https://rubygems.org/pages/download`.

Now, the gems should be installed! Now if you launch tmux, you'll be in maximum-awesome's configuration.

 Also, be forewarned that loading maximum-awesome can wipe out your locally configured `.tmux.conf` file (since the whole point, in essence, is that it is an awesome `.tmux.conf` file).

So be sure to back up your `.tmux.conf` file before running this command.

Using tmuxinator to make session management easier

In *Chapter 5*, *Diving Deeper*, we touched a bit on starting tmux with some default session configuration in the *Launch with defaults* section.

You may have noticed that even a rather simple configuration turned out to be a bit complex and tricky. This is one of those areas of core tmux that leaves a little to be desired.

Thankfully, the open source world has stepped up to the plate and created an excellent utility called *tmuxinator* to make this kind of configuration far simpler.

Built in ruby, tmuxinator is easy to install and provides a ton of useful capability. It does so by allowing you to specify in a simple and intuitive YAML syntax how you'd like your window laid out, any programs that should be run on launch, and more. tmuxinator allows you to create hooks that run before any window configuration is run and makes it much, much easier to specify a set of default windows and panes than in core tmux.

Let's run through the workflow of installing and creating a sample tmuxinator configuration file.

Installing tmuxinator

Since it is built in ruby, it's available as a ruby gem so installation is a breeze. In a command line, simply run:

```
$ gem install tmuxinator
```

> Depending on your system setup, you may have to use sudo to install gems. We'd suggest trying without sudo first, then falling back to it if the installation fails.

tmuxinator helpfully tells us during install that it includes a `tmuxinator doctor` command that can be used to check your local system configuration and ensure all is well. We recommend running that now and fixing any issues it finds:

```
$ tmuxinator doctor
```

When you see all items confirmed as **Yes**, you can move on.

Understanding the tmuxinator configuration

First, open a terminal and run the following command to create the initial tmuxinator configuration file:

```
$ tmuxinator new tutorial
```

The `tmuxinator new` command will start a new tmuxinator configuration file and we gave it the name `tutorial`. Feel free to name your file whatever you'd like of course.

You'll be dropped right into your editor of choice with the default contents of a tmuxinator configuration file already in your editor. A few things to note about this file:

- It is located in `~/.tmuxinator/<name>.yml` (in our case `~/tmuxinator/tutorial.yml`). This is where tmuxinator will store all of its configuration files. This is nice because you can have multiple configuration files and they will all live in one place and be accessible by tmuxinator.

- After a couple lines, there are a bunch of comments. These comments indicate options that could be used but aren't by default. We will dig into these in a bit.

- At the bottom of the file is the YAML that actually lays out the windows, panes, and so on. tmuxinator includes a default set of layouts.

tmuxinator includes its own kind of domain-specific language to build a rich configuration of windows, panes, and the default programs to run in them.

For example, what follows is a sample configuration file. We have added useful comments starting with # before each line to describe what the following line is doing:

```
# sets the name for this tmuxinator config
name: tutorial
# sets the root directory, all new panes will start with a
# terminal opened to this directory
root: ~/

# this is the start of the specification for which windows
windows:
  # this specifies the first window named "editor"
  - editor:
    # the "editor" window should have a vertical layout
    layout: main-vertical
    # this specifies that the "editor" window should have two
    # panes
    panes:
      # emacs should be running in one pane
      - emacs
      # top should be running in the other pane
      - top
# now we have a second window called "server" that should start
# running the command "node ~/myapp.js" on opening
- server: node ~/myapp.js
# there should be a third window called "logs" which should
# start with the tail command to view the logs
- logs: tail -f log/development.log
```

This is a very succinct way to specify some very complex behavior for windows and panes! Feel free to make any tweaks you would like to the file and save it. Now to start it, simply run:

```
$ tmuxinator start tutorial
```

Again, `tutorial` could be replaced with your filename. You'll see tmux is launched, but not only did it launch, but it also opened multiple windows and it has the name you gave it in the bottom left hand corner! If you open a new window, it should open to the root path specified in your configuration file, and so on.

So how does this black magic work you may wonder? Well under the hood it's a bunch of ruby scripts that start tmux and set it all up for you using the configuration YAML to guide that setup.

Revisiting the commented lines

Going back to the configuration file, there were some commented lines at the top that we said we'd dig into later. Well here we are! Let's dig in.

In the following code snippet we've copied the comment chunk from the top of the default tmuxinator configuration file:

```
# Optional tmux socket
# socket_name: foo

# Runs before everything. Use it to start daemons etc.
# pre: sudo /etc/rc.d/mysqld start

# Runs in each window and pane before window/pane specific commands.
Useful for setting up interpreter versions.
# pre_window: rbenv shell 2.0.0-p247

# Pass command line options to tmux. Useful for specifying a different
tmux.conf.
# tmux_options: -f ~/.tmux.mac.conf

# Change the command to call tmux.  This can be used by derivatives/
wrappers like byobu.
# tmux_command: byobu
```

You will see that there are comments to help explain the commands but let's go into a bit more depth.

We have not yet discussed sockets much as we get into rather esoteric territory, but the first line allows you to specify a socket name.

By default, when tmux is first launched, a server is launched on the machine and that server creates a socket on which it begins listening. Then the client is launched and connects to that socket. This is all rather seamless under normal usage.

This socket persisting is what allows you to detach the tmux session and reattach it. In reality, when you detach you are terminating the client; however, the tmux server continues humming along, listening on that socket for incoming connections. When you decide to reattach to a session, you are launching a client and connecting to that socket.

This socket is also what allows multiple people to connect to a single tmux session as we saw in *Chapter 6, tmux for SSH, Pair Programming, and More*, when we discussed using tmux for pair programming.

So far, whenever we ran a tmux command to connect, we seamlessly connected to that default socket, but you can launch tmux and specify your own socket path or name. This will allow us to run more than one independent instance of tmux on the same machine.

So, this configuration option allows us to specify the socket name when we launch with `tmuxinator start <name>`.

The next section starting with the `pre` command is copied in the following code snippet:

```
# Runs before everything. Use it to start daemons etc.
# pre: sudo /etc/rc.d/mysqld start
```

This section allows you to specify any commands to run when the tmuxinator session is started as its name implies. This is great to start any background tasks that do not have a UI but which we would like to be running and available for the session. This is convenient because it prevents us from having to open a new pane (or panes), launch a program, then leave it around forever but just ignore it. The following code snippet allows us to specify tmux options specific to this tmuxinator instance that may not appear in the standard `.tmux.conf file`:

```
# Runs in each window and pane before window/pane specific commands.
Useful for setting up interpreter versions.
# pre_window: rbenv shell 2.0.0-p247
```

This command allows us to run a command with every window or pane that we create rather than just on tmux launch. In the following commands we're passing the configuration file:

```
# Pass command line options to tmux. Useful for specifying a different
tmux.conf.
# tmux_options: -f ~/.tmux.mac.conf
```

There could be simpler commands such as changing the prefix key or anything else we saw back in *Chapter 2, Configuring tmux* or more powerful as in the example where they are loading another configuration file and sucking in all of its commands. The following code allows us to change the command used to call tmux:

```
# Change the command to call tmux.  This can be used by derivatives/
wrappers like byobu.
# tmux_command: byobu
```

This code snippet mentions byobu, which is a program that basically sits atop tmux (or GNU Screen) and adds additional functionality to them. The idea behind this is that if you prefer to use tmuxinator to call some command other than tmux that wraps tmux, you can do so using this line.

Summarizing tmuxinator

In summary, tmuxinator is an extremely powerful program that adds a lot of useful features to tmux and will save any tmux user a lot of time, every time they have to relaunch tmux and get all set up with their environment.

Not only can it be a huge timesaver, but can also be incredibly helpful for beginners as it can act as training wheels until a tmux user has grown accustomed to all the nuances of creating windows and panes. As we saw in *Chapter 3, Sessions, Windows, and Panes*, creating and manipulating panes can be fairly difficult. Having a simple tmuxinator configuration file that can jumpstart that process without much effort can be incredibly helpful.

 For detailed command reference for tmuxinator, visit its project page on GitHub:

https://github.com/tmuxinator/tmuxinator

Using wemux to ease multiuser experience

Another fantastic utility built by the community is **wemux**. It seeks to simplify the multiuser experience in tmux. As we saw in the last chapter, setting tmux up for pair programming is an awesome feature of tmux. It builds upon that experience, making it easier to configure and adds some very useful functionality.

Jump on over to the wemux GitHub page to get started and install wemux:

`https://github.com/zolrath/wemux`

If you are in an active tmux session, detach it before proceeding with <Prefix>, *d*.

Now let's jump into wemux. From your terminal, run the following command:

`$ wemux start`

Boom! But wait, you may say that this looks exactly like tmux. You would be right, wemux is a wrapper around tmux so it is the tmux you know and love with some special sauce added to facilitate some of the multi-user concepts.

From your command line, run the following command:

`$ wemux users`

The output of this command can be seen in the following screenshot:

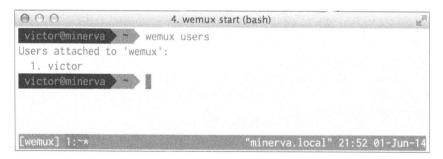

You should see a list containing one user. As you can imagine, if you had other users connected, they would appear in this list. Moreover, if there were another user in that list and we wanted to boot them out of our current wemux session, you could run the following command:

`$ wemux kick username`

This will boot `username` out of this wemux session. We can also configure wemux much as we did tmuxinator. First, we need to detach the current wemux session with <Prefix>, *d* and then run the command:

```
$ wemux config
```

It will open your configured editor to the wemux configuration file. You'll notice that most of it is commented out but there are very detailed comments that describe what each line does. Since it is so well commented, we won't go into great detail about each item.

Explaining the wemux modes

At a high level though, some of the coolest things about wemux are its modes. It has three modes:

- **Mirror mode**: This mode allows clients to attach to a wemux session read-only. This is great if you want to share your session but have no ability to edit anything in your session.

- **Pair mode**: This mode allows clients to attach and for all clients to share the same view and even the same cursor. This is great for many pair programming setups where either user should be able to touch the code and you want both users seeing the same view.

- **Rogue mode**: This mode allows multiple clients to attach and each be connected to the same tmux session, but both be able to have separate cursors and even open different windows. This is ideal when multiple people have to share a tmux session, but don't both need to be looking at the same thing.

Explaining other wemux additions to tmux

In addition to the modes, the user list, and the ability to kick users that wemux adds over tmux core, wemux also includes a user list you can add to your tmux status bar. It will display messages when users connect, and you can use wemux to connect to a remote server.

When you configure wemux, you are configuring the behavior of the server. Then clients can connect in one of the three modes, assuming, of course, you have enabled that mode on the server.

So, if you have configured your server in mirror mode only, a client will be able to connect via mirror mode (using `wemux mirror`) but will not be able to connect in rogue mode (using `wemux rogue`).

Using wemux is a fantastic way to streamline and tame the tmux multi-user experience.

Listing other tools to be used with tmux

Pairing down the preceding list of other tools to be used with tmux was incredibly difficult. We tried to discuss the most popular of each flavor but there are countless others.

One of the greatest strengths of tmux is the incredibly vibrant developer community, which has resulted in many great tools that work with tmux to enhance and extend the tmux experience.

For instance, the excellent Teamocil (`http://teamocil.com/`) is somewhat similar to tmuxinator in that they are both tmux configuration helpers that use YAML-based configuration files and ruby to configure tmux. We would have loved to discuss both, but since they are similar in many ways, it seemed like it could confuse our readers. We urge you to take a look at it if you have interest, as there are benefits of using one over the other and vice versa. A lot of it comes down to personal preference and taste.

Along with Teamocil, there are countless others, including vim-slime, tmuxp, tmuxifier, and many other excellent projects that extend tmux and add additional functionalities that can be incredibly useful in certain contexts. In the time between when this book was being written and when it is read there are likely others that have popped up and grown.

Perhaps you have noticed something about tmux that could use some optimizing and, equipped with the knowledge from this book, can start your own open source project extending tmux and furthering the community.

Summary

In this chapter, we learned about a handful of very useful third-party tools that can be used to extend the power and functionality of tmux. From turbocharging our configuration with *maximum-awesome* to a simpler and cleaner session management with tmuxinator and better pair programming with wemux, we had a nice taste of some really awesome utilities that improve upon and enhance the core features of tmux.

You may notice that while you learned a lot of different things throughout this book, when you sit down in front of your screen with an empty terminal window, your fingers may not know what to press to make things happen. For instance, you may remember that there is a way to split the current window into two panes horizontally, but may not remember the keystroke. This is expected! Unless you are a prodigy, one run through these concepts and keys will not solidify things entirely.

One learning trick that is very helpful is to choose three items to integrate into your workflow each week. Write the key combinations and descriptions of those items on an index card, place it by your computer, and try to integrate them into your workflow. By the end of the week, you will probably be able to drop the index card for those items and start anew.

Of course, there will be commands you forget or need to look up. For this, we have placed a comprehensive list of all new commands learned in each chapter at the end of the book. This way, you can immediately jump to the commands themselves without having to sift through all of the explanations we provided the first time you went through the text.

While we tried our best to give an overview of everything you would need to use tmux, there were inevitably some things we were unable to cover in this book. For everything else, the tmux man page we have mentioned many times throughout this book is the ultimate, exhaustive resource for the available tmux commands and key combinations.

So, we come to the end of our journey. We hope you have enjoyed learning about tmux with this book.

Appendix

The appendix will cover the following three topics:

- Why tmux?
- The configuration reference
- Key binding and command reference

Why tmux?

Many developers spend much of their day in a terminal. Whether using it for coding; SSH sessions to remote servers; browsing the filesystem; local tasks such as checking, compiling, or linting code, running unit tests; or even for mail or Internet Relay Chat (IRC), the terminal is one of the most widely used weapons in the developer's arsenal.

tmux is a command-line application that runs within your terminal and turbocharges it. Its powerful features allow for the simplification of many everyday tasks, as illustrated throughout this book. However, the main reason most people use a program like tmux is that it allows you to take a single terminal window and turn it into many virtual windows, each having their own state. It is one in a class of applications called **terminal multiplexers** (tmux is just a shortening of this term). It has some brethren, but the most prominent is GNU Screen.

Remember browsing in web browsers without tabs? If you answered no, you weren't missing much, and enjoy your youth! However, if you answered yes, it might take you a second to remember how much less convenient it was. Sure, there was nothing you can do with multiple tabs that you couldn't with no tabs and many browser windows, but it was still a very helpful boost to productivity to be able to group them together. Having many browser windows got very confusing. The advent of tabs allowed you to separate your browsing experience logically. Before tabs you would have had one browser window for reference documents, another for shopping, and so on.

Likewise, a terminal multiplexer such as tmux allows you to do the same, logically grouping multiple windows into a single terminal window, like tabs in a browser. Just as each browser tab contains its own state, so does each tmux window.

However, unlike browser tabs, which mostly just add organization, tmux actually adds a rich set of additional functionality to the terminal. Not only does tmux allow for dividing a window into panes so that multiple different bits of content can be on the screen at the same time, but tmux also adds *Copy mode* and other constructs that allow heavy terminal users to do more without leaving tmux or even having to reach for their mouse as often. We touch on many of these benefits throughout this book, so it's unnecessary to repeat them here.

Why use a terminal multiplexer over a standard terminal app with native tabs (for example, OS X Terminal, iTerm, Gnome Terminal, and so on)? There are many reasons, but the following are a few:

- The addition of Copy mode allows for copying and pasting between terminal windows without reaching for your mouse. This is not something that can be easily achieved with a standard tabbed terminal application.

- The addition of the saved state means that you can close a terminal window that is running tmux, and your entire session state will be saved and can be reattached later (assuming your terminal program allows the tmux server to continue running in the background; not all do). Any programs that were running continue running in the background. This is not the case with tabs in iTerm, OS X Terminal, or any Linux terminal. Closing one of these will drop your state for that window.

- There is much more power and flexibility to using tmux to split a window into panes and rearranging those panes than in using any tabbed terminal interface. Most modern terminal applications will now support simply a vertical or horizontal split, and that's about it. With tmux, the possibilities are (nearly) endless in terms of the number of splits, layouts, and so on.

- All of the tmux keyboard shortcuts for changing the size and layout of these splits translate into less dependence on your mouse, which is something most normal tabbed terminal applications cannot offer.

- Not only are there more shortcuts with tmux for tweaking the size of this or that, but tmux also offers a much broader range of customizability in terms of keyboard shortcuts for every operation it can handle. Literally, every single tmux shortcut can be changed or rewired with a simple configuration file, as shown in *Chapter 2, Configuring tmux*. Some terminal applications might offer some customization, but none are quite as powerful as tmux in this regard.

- The addition of capabilities in pair programming, setup configuration, and third-party utilities, as we discuss throughout this book, is unachievable with a standard terminal application.

Of course, the list goes on, as you have seen or will see throughout this book, but these are some of the highlights as to why a terminal multiplexer is preferred over a regular terminal app with tabs.

Now that you are most likely sold on using a terminal multiplexer rather than just tabs in a terminal program, why choose tmux over its main competitor, GNU Screen (Screen hereafter)? There are many reasons, but the following are a few:

- The tmux Command mode was written in order to allow other utilities to control tmux. This is the reason for the rich developer community that has sprung up around it. Screen is more difficult and complicated to control remotely.

- As a result, the third-party tools for working with tmux are much more prevalent and powerful.

- The tmux commands are simple utilities, taking a very good page from the UNIX playbook. These small commands can be run via key combinations, by entering the command after the tmux utility, or via tmux's Command mode. Screen is more of a monolith without these nicely separated commands.

- tmux is newer project, often learning from Screen's mistakes. The first Screen release was way back in 1987. The first tmux release was 22 years later in 2009.

- The tmux source has fewer lines of code while offering more features.

- Screen has been a mostly abandoned project for many years. In fact, there was not even a single minor Screen release between 2008 and April, 2014. It had been dormant since before tmux was released and finally had a minor release six years after the last one.

- tmux has a clean client-server model that allows tmux to keep running when you detach a tmux session. While you can detach from Screen, it has a less defined client-server model.

- Screen has, essentially, one set of key bindings. In contrast, tmux tries to stay more friendly to developers and includes both vi and Emacs key bindings for most of its commands.

- The pane and window management in tmux is much simpler and more powerful. With tmux, it is easy to split a window into many different panes, move them around, attach them to different windows, move windows, attach windows to different sessions, and so on. Many of these tasks are not possible in Screen, and they end up being far more complex than they are with tmux.

- The tmux status bar configuration, out of the box, is quite simple and defaults to what most people would like. Screen, on the other hand, does not include a status bar by default, and the way to specify it is very complex. For example, this is an actual line from my Screen configuration to enable a tmux-style status bar:

```
hardstatus string '%{= kG}[ %{G}%H %{g}[%{=kw}%?%-Lw%?%{r}(%{W}%n*
%f%t%?(%u)%?%{r})%{w}%?%+Lw%?%= %{g}] [%{B}%Y-%m-%d %{W}%c %{g}]'
```

No; this is not a joke. This is the actual line and all it does is display the same things that the tmux status bar supports out of the box.

There are more benefits of tmux over Screen, but this should give any reader a good indication of the rationale here.

As it was the first terminal multiplexer we ever used, Screen still has a special place in the author's heart. The intent here is certainly not to bash Screen, which, impressively, is celebrating its 27th year at the time of writing this. Screen is still quite a great program and very much paved the way for tmux. However, you purchased this book because you wanted to learn about tmux and our intent was to enumerate some reasons why tmux is the most awesome program of its type.

The configuration reference

What follows is the configuration file that we built over the course of *Chapter 2, Configuring tmux*:

```
# Enable mouse mode for mouse scrolling (tmux 1.9a+)
set-window-option -g mouse-mode on
# Enable mouse for selecting the window by clicking on the title
# in the status bar
set-option -g mouse-select-window on
# Enable mouse for selecting the pane by clicking on it
set-option -g mouse-select-pane on
# Enable the mouse for clicking and dragging to resize panes
set-option -g mouse-resize-pane on
```

```
# Set the status bar background to blue
set-option -g status-bg blue
# Set the status bar text to white
set-option -g status-fg white

# Widen the status-left a bit to fit more
set-option -g status-left-length 25
# Change status-left to be {username@host}
set-option -g status-left "{#(whoami)@#H}"

# Set the active window background in the status bar
set-window-option -g window-status-current-bg magenta

# Rebind the prefix key
set-option -g prefix C-t

# Add a key binding for reloading our configuration
bind-key C-r source-file ~/.tmux.conf
# Double tapping the prefix jumps to last window
bind-key C-t last-window

# Set escape time to not break vim
set-option -s escape-time 0

# Set the base-index to 1 rather than 0
set-option -g base-index 1
set-window-option -g pane-base-index 1

# Extend the display time to 2 seconds
set-option -g display-time 2000

# Store more history in the buffer than default
set-option -g history-limit 10000
```

Key binding and command reference

This is not intended as an exhaustive reference on tmux key bindings and commands. For that, view the tmux manual page by typing the following in your terminal:

```
$ man tmux
```

You can also view more information on tmux by visiting http://man.cx/tmux.

This is, instead, a chapter-by-chapter reference for the tmux keys and commands mentioned in each chapter along with a small description of what they do in the order in which they are mentioned.

This makes it easy to review and recall these key bindings and commands in the same order that they were covered in the chapter without having to wade through all of the text of that chapter.

Chapter 1 – Jump Right In

In this chapter, we jumped right in and went on a tour of many of the features of tmux. As a result, the following list of commands is widely varied:

- Launch tmux: `$ tmux`

- Rename a session: `$ tmux rename-session {session name}`

- Create a new window: <Prefix>, *c*

- Switch to the last window: <Prefix>, *l*

- Switch to a window by its index: <Prefix>, {index of window}

- List all key bindings: <Prefix>, *?*

- Initiate a search within the key bindings list: *Ctrl* + *s* (or / for vi users)

- Close any dialog opened by tmux, such as the key bindings list: *q*

- Open the choose window interface: <Prefix>, *w*

- Switch to the next window (by the window index): <Prefix>, *n*

- Switch to the previous window (by the window index): <Prefix>, *p*

- Find an open window with the specified search text: <Prefix>, *f*

- Detach the current tmux session: <Prefix>, *d*

- List all active sessions: `$ tmux list-sessions`

- Start tmux and attach a session by name: `$ tmux attach-session -t {session-name}`

- A shorter way to start tmux and attach a session: `$ tmux attach -t {session-name}`

- An even shorter way to start tmux and attach a session (only works when there is a single active session): `$ tmux attach`

- List all active sessions' aliases: `$ tmux ls`

- List all tmux commands: `$ tmux list-commands`

- List all tmux commands' aliases: `$ tmux lscm`

- Rename the current window: <Prefix>, ,
- Kill the current window: <Prefix>, &

Chapter 2 – Configuring tmux

In this chapter, we dealt a lot with configuration. Listed here are the key bindings and commands introduced in *Chapter 2, Configuring tmux*, but see the *Configuration reference* section for information on the new configuration items we discussed:

- Set a tmux option: `$ tmux set-option {option to set} {value}`
- Disable the status bar: `$ tmux set-option status off`
- Enable the status bar: `$ tmux set-option status on`
- See whether you are in the Emacs or vi mode: `$ tmux show-options -g | grep key`
- Reload the tmux configuration: `$ tmux source-file ~/.tmux.conf`
- Show all previously displayed messages: <Prefix>, ~

Chapter 3 – Sessions, Windows, and Panes

In *Chapter 3, Sessions, Windows, and Panes*, we learned all about how to move and organize your content within a terminal window using the three core building blocks of tmux: sessions, windows, and panes. As a result, the key commands we learned throughout this chapter relate to manipulating one of those three items. The key commands covered in this chapter are as follows:

- Launch tmux with a named session: `$ tmux new-session -s {session name}`
- Access the switch session interactive dialog: <Prefix>, *s*
- Switch to the next session: <Prefix>, *)*
- Switch to the previous session: <Prefix>, *(*
- Split a pane into two panes (horizontally): <Prefix>, %
- Switch the cursor to the other pane: <Prefix>, *o*
- Move the cursor to the pane to the right, left, down, or up: <Prefix>, right arrow; <Prefix>, left arrow; <Prefix>, down arrow; <Prefix>, up arrow
- Kill the current pane: <Prefix>, *x*
- Split a pane into two panes (vertically): <Prefix>, "
- Resize the current pane: <Prefix>, *Alt* + {arrow key}

- Resize the current pane in 1 cell steps: <Prefix>, *Ctrl* + {arrow key}
- View current pane indexes: <Prefix>, *q*
- Switch to the pane by index: <Prefix>, *q*, {index of pane}
- Cycle through pane layouts: <Prefix>, *Space*
- Switch to the `even-horizontal` pane layout: <Prefix>, *Meta* + *1*
- Switch to the `even-vertical` pane layout: <Prefix>, *Meta* + *2*
- Switch to the `main-horizontal` pane layout: <Prefix>, *Meta* + *3*
- Switch to the `main-vertical` pane layout: <Prefix>, *Meta* + *4*
- Switch to the `tile` pane layout: <Prefix>, *Meta* + *5*

Chapter 4 – Manipulating Text

We spent this chapter learning about Copy mode, paste buffers, and other concepts related to text manipulation.

- Clear the tmux history: `$ tmux clear-history`
- Enter Copy mode: <Prefix>, *[*
- Enter Command mode: <Prefix>, *:*
- Enter Clock mode: <Prefix>, *t*
- View the Emacs key bindings for Copy mode: `tmux list-keys -t emacs-copy`
- View the vi key bindings for Copy mode: `tmux list-keys -t vi-copy`

Many of the following commands are valid only after entering Copy mode. We will start these commands with *[CM]* to indicate that Copy mode should be activated first.

This is also the first command set that really has two different modes, Emacs and vi mode. As such, each command actually has two different key bindings, depending on your chosen mode. We will display the default key binding *(Emacs)* first, and then we will display the alternative *(vi)* in parentheses.

For the Emacs key bindings, many involve the key *Meta*, which is often bound to the *Alt / Option* key and is a key to which any Emacs user should be accustomed.

We discussed how to set the mode keys as Emacs or vi back in *Chapter 2, Configuring tmux*.

- [CM] Scroll up by page: *Page Up* or *Meta + v* (*Ctrl + b*)
- [CM] Scroll down by page: *Page Down* or *Ctrl + v* (*Ctrl + f*)
- [CM] Move the cursor up: up arrow or *Ctrl + p* (*k*)
- [CM] Move the cursor down: down arrow or *Ctrl + n* (*j*)
- [CM] Move the cursor left: left arrow or *Ctrl + b* (*h*)
- [CM] Move the cursor right: right arrow or *Ctrl + f* (*l*)
- [CM] Jump to top of window history: *Meta + >* (*g*)
- [CM] Jump to bottom of window history: *Meta + <* (*G*)
- [CM] Search up: *Ctrl + r* (*?*)
- [CM] Search down: *Ctrl + s* (*/*)
- [CM] Jump to a specific line: *g* (*:*)
- [CM] Exit Copy mode: *q* (*Esc*)
- [CM] Start the selection for copying: *Ctrl* + Space bar (Space bar)
- [CM] Copy the selection to the paste buffer: *Meta + w* (*Enter*)
- [CM] Toggle the rectangular selection: *R* (*v*)
- Paste the text from the paste buffer: <Prefix>,]
- Open the interactive paste buffer chooser: <Prefix>, =
- List all buffers for viewing only: <Prefix>, :, list + buffers, *Enter*

Chapter 5 – Diving Deeper

In this chapter, we went a bit more in depth on a smorgasbord of topics. As a result, our keyboard commands and configuration items for this chapter are quite widely varied over a range of tmux capabilities:

- Enter Command mode: <Prefix>, :
- Open the interactive paste buffer chooser: <Prefix>, =
- Save the paste buffer to a path: `save-buffer -b {buffer index} {file path}`
- Load the paste buffer from a file: `load-buffer {file-path}`
- Set a paste buffer directly: `set-buffer "{text to set in buffer}"`
- Capture contents of the current pane to the paste buffer: `capture-pane`
- View the contents of the most recently copied paste buffer: `show-buffer`

- View the contents of a paste buffer by index: `show-buffer -b {index}`
- Delete the last copied item from the paste buffer: <Prefix>, -
- Delete items from the paste buffer by index: `delete-buffer -b {index}`
- Clear the tmux history for the current pane: `clear-history`
- Clear the tmux history for a pane by index: `clear-history -t {index}`
- Move the window from one session to another: `move-window` or <Prefix>, .
- Link a window between two sessions: `link-window -t {target session}`
- Unlink the window from the current session: `unlink-window`
- Break the current pane from the current window: <Prefix>, !
- Break a pane into its own window: `break-pane -s {session}:{window}.{pane}`
- Join the current pane to a target window: `join-pane -t {session}:{window}`
- Join a pane to a target window: `join-pane -s {session}:{window}.{pane} -t {session}:{window}`

Index

E

Emacs mode 16, 27, 28
Emacs-style key bindings, Copy mode 66

F

file
    paste buffer, loading from 76, 77
    paste buffer, saving to 75, 76
foreground color
    modifying, of status bar 32

G

grouped sessions
    used, for pairing 100, 101

H

handy configuration tips
    about 43
    base index, starting at 1 46
    display time, lengthening 45, 46
    double tapping of prefix key, binding to
        last-window 43
    escape time, modifying 44
    history limit, lengthening 44
Homebrew
    URL 104

I

installation, tmuxinator 107
items
    selecting, from paste buffer 71

K

key binding
    about 121
    help page 15-17
keys
    unbinding 40

L

link-window command 84
load-buffer [path] command 76

M

man page
    accessing 47
    reference, for example 47, 66
Mirror mode, wemux 113
modes, tmux
    Clock mode 64
    Command mode 63
    Control mode 64
    Copy mode 63
    Default mode 63
modes, wemux
    Mirror 113
    Pair 113
    Rogue 113
mouse modes
    enabling 28
multiple panes
    working with 54-56
multiple sessions
    working with 53

O

option types 42, 43
OS X Pasteboard
    tmux, using with 103-105

P

Pair mode, wemux 113
pair programming, tmux
    about 96
    connecting to same session, locally 96, 97
    grouped sessions, using 100, 101
    Vagrant Cloud, for better security pair
        programming 98-100
pane contents
    capturing, in paste buffer 78
pane layouts
    cycling through 58, 59
panes
    benefits 52
    breaking 85
    joining 85, 86
    operations 59
    overview 51

Thank you for buying
Getting Started with tmux

About Packt Publishing

Packt, pronounced 'packed', published its first book "*Mastering phpMyAdmin for Effective MySQL Management*" in April 2004 and subsequently continued to specialize in publishing highly focused books on specific technologies and solutions.

Our books and publications share the experiences of your fellow IT professionals in adapting and customizing today's systems, applications, and frameworks. Our solution based books give you the knowledge and power to customize the software and technologies you're using to get the job done. Packt books are more specific and less general than the IT books you have seen in the past. Our unique business model allows us to bring you more focused information, giving you more of what you need to know, and less of what you don't.

Packt is a modern, yet unique publishing company, which focuses on producing quality, cutting-edge books for communities of developers, administrators, and newbies alike. For more information, please visit our website: www.packtpub.com.

About Packt Open Source

In 2010, Packt launched two new brands, Packt Open Source and Packt Enterprise, in order to continue its focus on specialization. This book is part of the Packt Open Source brand, home to books published on software built around Open Source licenses, and offering information to anybody from advanced developers to budding web designers. The Open Source brand also runs Packt's Open Source Royalty Scheme, by which Packt gives a royalty to each Open Source project about whose software a book is sold.

Writing for Packt

We welcome all inquiries from people who are interested in authoring. Book proposals should be sent to author@packtpub.com. If your book idea is still at an early stage and you would like to discuss it first before writing a formal book proposal, contact us; one of our commissioning editors will get in touch with you.

We're not just looking for published authors; if you have strong technical skills but no writing experience, our experienced editors can help you develop a writing career, or simply get some additional reward for your expertise.

Learning Cython Programming

ISBN: 978-1-78328-079-7   Paperback: 110 pages

Expand your existing legacy applications in C using Python

1. Extend C applications with pure Python code.

2. Expand low-level C open source projects with pure Python – Tmux.

3. Get the most out of highly computational Python code using Cython.

4. Integrate your C applications with Python Distutils and Automake/Autoconf.

Getting Started with oVirt 3.3

ISBN: 978-1-78328-007-0   Paperback: 140 pages

A practical guide to successfully implementing and calibrating oVirt 3.3, a feature-rich open source server virtualization platform

1. Understand and master the internal arrangement of oVirt.

2. Quickly install and configure the oVirt virtualization environment.

3. Create your own infrastructure using the data centers, clusters, and networks within oVirt.

Please check **www.PacktPub.com** for information on our titles

Apache Solr PHP Integration

ISBN: 978-1-78216-492-0   Paperback: 118 pages

Build a fully-featured and scalable search application using PHP to unlock the search functions provided by Solr

1. Understand the tools that can be used to communicate between PHP and Solr, and how they work internally.

2. Explore the essential search functions of Solr such as sorting, boosting, faceting, and highlighting using your PHP code.

3. Take a look at some advanced features of Solr such as spell checking, grouping, and auto complete with implementations using PHP code.

Learning Shell Scripting with Zsh

ISBN: 978-1-78328-293-7   Paperback: 132 pages

Your one-stop guide to reading, writing, and debugging simple and complex Z shell scripts

1. A step-by-step guide that will show you how to use zsh and its repertoire of powerful features to improve the efficiency of your daily tasks.

2. Learn how to configure and use zsh.

3. Discover some advanced features of zsh such as process and parameter substitution, running on restricted functionality mode, and emulating other shells.

Please check **www.PacktPub.com** for information on our titles

www.ingramcontent.com/pod-product-compliance
Lightning Source LLC
LaVergne TN
LVHW081345050326
832903LV00024B/1326